Nelson
Spelling ❸

Louis Quildon

Series Authors
Donna Duplak
Deb Kekewich
Jim Kekewich
Clare Kosnik
Louis Quildon
Edgar Schmidt
Catherine Walker

Clare Kosnik, Senior Author

I(T)P® Nelson

an International Thomson Publishing company

Toronto • Albany • Bonn • Boston • Cincinnati • Detroit • London • Madrid • Melbourne
Mexico City • New York • Pacific Grove • Paris • San Francisco • Singapore • Tokyo • Washington

I(T)P® **International Thomson Publishing**
     The ITP logo is a trademark under licence

Published in 1997 by
I(T)P® **Nelson**
A division of Thomson Canada Limited
1120 Birchmount Road
Scarborough, Ontario M1K 5G4
Visit our Website at **http://www.nelson.com/nelson.html**

ISBN 0-17-606557-1

Canadian Cataloguing in Publication Data

Quildon, Louis
    Nelson Spelling 3

ISBN 0-17-606557-1

1. Spellers.   2. English language – Orthography
and spelling – Problems, exercises, etc.   I. Title

PE1145.2.Q52 1997   428.1   C97-930020-7

Team Leader/Publisher: Mark Cobham
Project Editor: Jennifer Rowsell
Series Editor: Joanne Close
Series Designer: Peggy Rhodes
Cover Illustrator: Per-Henrik Gurth
Senior Composition Analyst: Marnie Benedict
Production Coordinator: Donna Brown
Permissions: Vicki Gould
Film: Imaging Excellence
Photography: Ray Boudreau

Printed and bound in Canada by Metropole Litho

Acknowledgements
Permissions to reprint copyright material is
gratefully acknowledged. Every reasonable effort
to trace the copyright holders of materials
appearing in this book has been made.
Information that will enable the publisher to
rectify any error or ommission will be welcomed.

"Unfair" by Loris Lesynski, author/illustrator of
"Boy Soup." Reprinted with permission; "Stomp"
by Loris Lesynski, author/illustrator of "Boy
Soup." Reprinted with permission; "Tree House"
by Shel Silverstein from "Where The Sidewalk
Ends" by Shel Silverstein. Copyright © 1974 by
Evil Eye Music, Inc. Reprinted with permission
of HarperCollins Publishers; "Shiny" by James
Reeves from *Wandering Moon* published by
William Heinemann Ltd.; "What's In The Sack"
by Shel Silverstein from "Where The Sidewalk
Ends" by Shel Silverstein. Copyright © 1974 by
Evil Eye Music, Inc. Reprinted with permission
of HarperCollins Publishers; "Balloons" from
Merry Go Day, copyright © 1991 text by Sheree
Fitch, illustrations by Molly Bobak. Reprinted
with permission of Doubleday Canada Limited.

Illustrators
The authors and publisher gratefully acknowledge
the contributions of the following illustrators:
Sean Dawdy, Daniel Dumont, Norman Eyolfson,
Dusan Petricic, and Sue Truman.

Reviewers
The author and publisher gratefully acknowledge the contributions of the following educators:

Diane Assinger	Christine Finnochio	Lenora Higgs	Josephine Scott
Red Deer, AB	Stoney Creek, ON	Canterbury, NB	Guelph, ON
Halina Bartley	Doreen Grey	Jennette MacKenzie	Maureen Skinner
Peterborough, ON	Calgary, AB	Hamilton, ON	Scarborough, ON
Eleanor Creasey	Lynne Healy	Lori Rog	Mary Tarasoff
Calgary, AB	Lower Sackville, NS	Regina, SK	Victoria, BC
Dena Domijan			
Burnaby, BC			

1 2 3 4 5 ML 01 00 99 98 97

Table of Contents

Lesson		Page

About Your Nelson Spelling Book

Here are some notes about your book. It includes many parts that help you learn about words and become a better speller.

Lessons

Each lesson looks at 1 spelling pattern. It opens with a poem, a story part, or a picture. The opener shows you words that share the lesson's spelling pattern.

2   bl, cl, fl

Creating Your Word List

Each lesson has a Word Box that contains 10 words. Use these words, the opener, and other words that share the same pattern to make your Lesson Word list. These are the words you will learn to spell. Sometimes you will find **challenge words**. These are words that many people find hard to spell.

Word Box

close
blend
flip
clue
floor
blow
clear
flies
block
flame

Spelling Strategy

Strategy Spot

Say Two Letters in a Blend

Each lesson includes a strategy to help you spell. These strategies are used by good spellers when they must spell new or difficult words. You can use the strategies when you write.

Zoom in on Your Words

Activities, puzzles, and games help you learn the meaning and spelling of your Lesson Words. You will practise your Lesson Words and learn new words.

Try This! is an extra challenge you may want to do.

Quick Tip

Some lessons include Quick Tips. These tips give you information about the spelling pattern.

Did You Know?

Other lessons include Did You Know? spots. These spots contain interesting information about words and their origins.

At Home activities and games can be done on your own or with a family member.

A flashback question is included at the end of each lesson. It asks you to think about what you have learned.

FOCUS ON LANGUAGE ▷ Compound Words

These pages give information and activities on many topics. You can learn when to capitalize letters, what nouns and verbs are, and how to make your writing even more exciting.

Connecting with...

Spelling is a part of all subjects. These pages include spelling information and activities in subjects like math, art, science, and media.

Spell Check

After every 5 lessons, you will do a Spell Check lesson. These lessons review patterns and strategies you have been learning. You will use the Lesson Words you still need to practise in games, puzzles, and other activities.

Short Vowel Sounds

Say this poem. Can you solve its puzzle?

First there was Arn, then
Ben and Cal, Dave and Ed
Fred and Gert, Hal and Ian
Jan and Kim, Lou and Moe

Along the way they met Norm, then
Orn and Pete, Quent and Roy
Sue and Tess, Uma and Val
Win and Xy, Yves and Zach

They thought they'd play baseball
Teams were even, teams were equal
Except one name that did not fit
Listen to the rhythm (there's your tip)

Word Box

upset
drift
pond
cost
sang
than
print
left
mess
running

Creating Your Word List

Say these words:

sang   mess   cost   drift   upset

Listen to the short sounds of the vowels (**a, e, i, o, u**).
Say the names in the poem again. Which names have
short vowel sounds?

1. Make a list of words that have short vowel sounds. You
can use the poem to help you get started. Print your
words in a chart like the one on the next page.

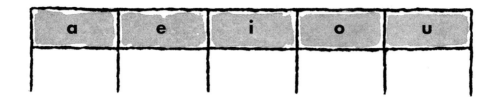

2. With your teacher, list the words you will be learning to spell. You can use: the Word Box, the poem, your own words. These are your Lesson Words.

3. **In your notebook**
   - Write your Lesson Words.
   - Say the words. Listen to their short vowel sounds.
   - Circle the short vowels.
   - Look at other letters in the words.

Strategy Spot

Learn About Spelling Strategies

There are many ways to learn how to spell. We call these ways spelling strategies. In each lesson, you will learn about a strategy you can use to help you spell new or hard words. You can use these strategies when you write stories, make lists, write invitations, and send letters.

Zoom in on Your Words

1. **Name Changes** Read the ABC poem at the beginning of the lesson. Change the names in the poem by using the names of students in your class. If no one in your class has a name that begins with one of the letters, like X, make up a name. Continue the poem until you have a name for each letter of the alphabet.

2. **A New Name** Write and say your first and last name. Mark the short vowels.

      a) Try to say your name without the vowels.

      b) Try to say your name without the consonants.

Try This! Imagine that you could pick a new name for yourself. What name would you pick? Tell a partner your choice and why you like this name.

3. **Draw and Write** Pick 3 Lesson Words. Draw a picture for 1 word. Write a sentence that includes the other 2 words. Share your work with a partner.

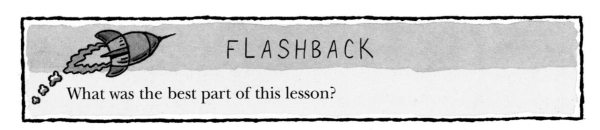

4. **Listen Carefully...** Find a partner. Take turns saying these sets of words. Listen for the word in each set that **does not** have a short sound.

pin	pine	pan	pun	pen
fun	fin	fine	fan	fawn
most	mast	must	mess	mist
pep	pop	pipe	pip	pup

5. **Scrambled Words** Some of the Word Box words have been scrambled. Can you unscramble them?

  a) nags   **b)** tocs   **c)** donp   **d)** stupe   **e)** felt

6. **Why Julie?** Ask your mother or father, or another family member, to tell you how you got your name. Share your story with the class.

FLASHBACK

What was the best part of this lesson?

SOCIAL STUDIES

Your Community

Look around your class. You go to school with many people. Other people, who are not in your class, are also an important part of your school community.

Go on a tour of your school with your teacher. Make a list of people who work there. You can ask their names and list some of the jobs they do.

With a partner, make a poster of your school and some of the students and staff. Label your poster and include the school's address, postal code, and phone number.

11

Look at the picture below. Find the names of things that begin with these letters: **bl**, **cl**, **fl**. (Hint: The names of 8 things begin with these letters.)

Word Box

close
blend
flip
clue
floor
blow
clear
flies
block
flame

Creating Your Word List

Say these words:

block   blend   flame   clear   flies

Listen to the way the first 2 letters in each word **blend** together.

1. Make a list of other **l** blend words. List your words in a chart like this one.

bl	cl	fl

2. With your teacher, list the words you will be learning to spell. You can use: the Word Box, the picture, your own words. These are your Lesson Words.

3. In your notebook
- Write your Lesson Words.
- Say each word and underline the l blend.

Strategy Spot

Say Two Letters in a Blend

Words that begin with an **l** blend are easy to misspell. Often we say the 2 letters together, gliding over the l. To help you spell blends, say the sounds of both the first *and* the second letter.

Zoom in on Your Words

1. Listen and Write Ask a partner to say your Lesson Words. Listen for the blend in each word. Write the 2 letters in the blend, then write the rest of the letters.

2. Word in a Word Look at the words in the Word Box to find these words.

a) or	**b)** am	**c)** low
d) end	**e)** lock	**f)** lend
g) ear	**h)** lose	**i)** lip

Write the words in your notebook. Underline the little words.

Try This! Pick 2 Lesson Words. How many smaller words can you find in them?

3. **Get in Shape**   In your notebook, match these wordprints with the Word Box words that fit them.

a) 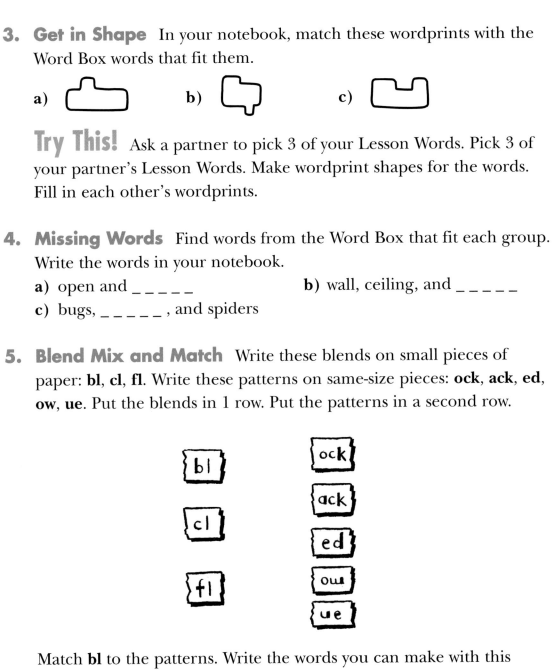   b)   c)

Try This!   Ask a partner to pick 3 of your Lesson Words. Pick 3 of your partner's Lesson Words. Make wordprint shapes for the words. Fill in each other's wordprints.

4. **Missing Words**   Find words from the Word Box that fit each group. Write the words in your notebook.

a) open and _ _ _ _ _   b) wall, ceiling, and _ _ _ _ _

c) bugs, _ _ _ _ _ , and spiders

5. **Blend Mix and Match**   Write these blends on small pieces of paper: **bl**, **cl**, **fl**. Write these patterns on same-size pieces: **ock**, **ack**, **ed**, **ow**, **ue**. Put the blends in 1 row. Put the patterns in a second row.

bl   ock

cl   ack

fl   ed

ow

ue

Match **bl** to the patterns. Write the words you can make with this combination. Do the same with **cl**, then **fl**. Which blend made the most words?

 6. **The Clue Was...**   Pick 5 Lesson Words. Use each word in a sentence. If you like, use more than 1 Lesson Word in a sentence. Share your writing with a family member.

FOCUS ON LANGUAGE ▷ Written Directions

This year you will do many spelling activities. You will do some on your own, some with a partner, and some as part of a group. In many activities, you will need to read and follow directions.

Here are some direction "words" that tell you what to do.

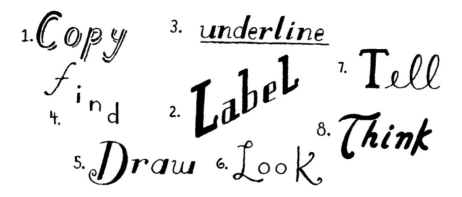

1. Copy
3. underline
7. Tell
4. find
2. Label
5. Draw
6. Look
8. Think

Follow these directions to complete this activity.

Directions

1. Turn to a new page in your notebook.

2. Write the date at the top of the page.

3. On the left-hand side of the pink line (margin), write **1**.

4. On the right-hand side of the margin, write **Copy**.

5. Draw a picture of what the word means.

6. Do the same for the other 7 direction words.

FLASHBACK

What is the most important thing you learned in this lesson?

What pictures do you see when you read these sentences?

In the ocean a crab crawls like a tractor in a forest of bright green seaweed. In the swamp a crocodile travels through the water like a ship sailing home.
Carl Amman

Word Box

grass
trip
crawl
frost
travel
friend
ground
crowd
trace
grandmother

Creating Your Word List

Say these words:

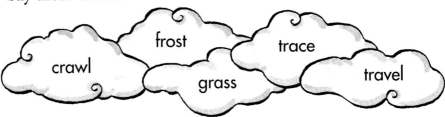

The first letter in each word is a consonant. Listen to how each consonant blends with **r** to form a new sound. We call this sound an **r** blend.

1. Make a list of **r** blend words you know.

2. With your teacher, list the words you will be learning to spell. You can use: the Word Box, the sentences, your own words. These are your Lesson Words.

3. **In your notebook**
   - Write your Lesson Words.
   - Say each word and underline the **r** blend.

Look for Blends at the Beginning of a Word

A blend, like **cr**, **fr**, **gr**, and **tr**, is usually found at the beginning of a word. When you are not sure how to spell a word, say it slowly. Listen for a blend at the start of a word. This can help you to start spelling it.

Zoom in on Your Words

1. **Underline Blends** Choose 5 Lesson Words. Write the words and underline the blends in each.

2. **A Travelling Crocodile** Read the sentences at the top of page 16. Draw a picture of how you see the crab or the crocodile. Look at a partner's picture. Tell your partner why you drew your picture the way you did.

3. **In Your Reading** Make a list of **r** blend words from a book you are reading. Choose 1 or 2 words. Draw a picture of each in your notebook.

4. **Mix and Match** Match the blends with the patterns. Write the words you make in your notebook. The first one has been done for you.

Blends	Patterns
tr ————————————	ost
cr ——————— ip	ip
fr	ound
gr	awl

17

5. Brass Grass Read each Lesson Word aloud. For each, try to find 1 rhyming word.

Try This! Draw or write 1 of your rhyming word pairs.

brass grass

6. Magic Squares Words in this Magic Square begin with **r** blends. In your notebook, write the words to make a magic square. An example has been done for you.

	Magic Square	
Example		**Words**
Fred	F R O G	bred
grim	R R	grip
drum	E I	brag
frog	D R U M	drop

Try This! Make these words form a magic square: *trust, front, treat, frost.*

R blends are usually at the beginning of a word. Sometimes they are in the middle of a word but they are **never** at the end.

QUICK TIP

7. Newspaper Search With a family member, make a list of **r** blend words you find in newspapers and magazines. Write the words in the correct column.

cr	fr	gr	tr
crash	fresh	grey	trailer

18

FOCUS ON LANGUAGE ▷ Personal Dictionaries

When you make a Personal Dictionary, you make a dictionary just for you. Since you are the only person who will use your dictionary, you decide which words to include. You can add:

- words that are hard to spell,
- words from a theme you are working on,
- words from your writing folder that give you trouble.

1. Label your first page **A**, your second page **B**, your third page **C**. Continue until you have labelled 26 pages – 1 page for each letter of the alphabet.

2. Go through your writing folder. Find 5 words that are hard for you to spell.

3. Write each word in your Personal Dictionary. Make sure that the words are written on the right page and that they are spelled correctly.

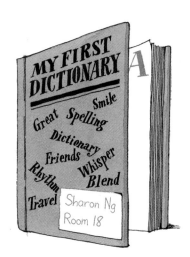

FLASHBACK

Where is a good place to keep your Personal Dictionary?

Read this poem. Do you have the same problem as the poet?

Unfair

I can't spell **kat**
    and I can't spell **chairr**.
I can't spell **appel** and
    I can't spell **per**.
But I can spell **belligerent**
    and **circumnavigation**
I can spell **kaleidoscope**
    caffeine
    and **fascination**.
Can I really *help* it
    if the words I spell the best
are never there among the ones
    that turn up on a test?

Loris Lesynski

Word Box

spill
snow
desk
whisper
smell
skunk
smile
snake
spend
snail

Creating Your Word List

Say these words:

skunk
desk
snake
smell
whisper

Listen to how **s** blends with the next consonant. The **s** blend can be at the beginning of a word, in the middle of a word, or at the end of a word.

1. Make a list of **s** blend words you know.

2. With your teacher, list the words you will be learning to spell. You can use: the Word Box, the poem, your own words. These are your Lesson Words.

3. **In your notebook**
   - Write your Lesson Words.
   - Say each word and underline the **s** blend.
   - Add **s** blend words to your Personal Dictionary. This will help you in your reading and writing.

Strategy Spot

Make a Foldover

Here is a fun way to practise spelling Lesson Words. It's called a **foldover**.

1. Pick a Lesson Word you want to practise.
2. Fold a piece of paper into thirds. This makes 3 rectangles.
3. Write your word in the top rectangle.
4. Fold over your writing.
5. Now write the word — without looking — in the third rectangle.
6. Open up the paper and check your spelling.
7. Using the same piece of paper, do this with 2 other Lesson Words.

Zoom in on Your Words

1. **Apply the Strategy** Follow the steps in the Strategy Spot to practise your Lesson Words.

2. Special Delivery Some words from the Word Box are missing from this letter. Write the missing words in your notebook.

Dear Aunt Stacy,
Thanks for asking me to __e__ summer on the farm again. I ___l_ when I think about how much fun we had last year. Can I bring Sarah again? I promise she won't chase a___n_ this time. Her sense of s____ is still not better. She says it doesn't matter. She likes __a__s this year and they don't smell. I can't wait for holidays to begin.
Your niece,
Natasha

3. Gone Fishing Work with a partner. Match each hook to the fish. How many words can you and your partner make?

Write each word you make. Trade lists with another pair of students. Add words they found to your list, then make a class list of words.

4. I Smile When Make a list of 5 things that make you smile. Ask a family member to record 5 things that make him or her smile. Trade your lists. Did you list some of the same things?

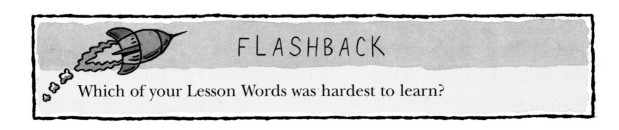

FLASHBACK

Which of your Lesson Words was hardest to learn?

Tongue Twisters

Say this nonsense sentence out loud three times. Each time, say the sentence faster.

Smart snakes sat on small snails with spurs

Tongue twisters are hard to say because most of the words have the same beginning sound. The faster you try to say them, the harder they are to say.

Make a group of 4 members. Look at the tongue twister at the top of the page, or find another tongue twister. Decide how you could present the tongue twister to other groups. You could:

- say the tongue twister as a chant,
- have each member say separate words,
- say the tongue twister in different voices,
- choral read the tongue twister.

Practise and plan your presentation. When you are ready, present your tongue twister to other groups.

For an extra challenge, write your own tongue twister. Use your name and add words that have the same beginning sound.

Have Fun!

Move in one spot to do the actions in this chant.

Stomp

Stomp up steps
   stomp back down
      one stomp sideways
         one stomp around.

Tiptoe up
   tiptoe down
      one tip sideways
         tiptoe around.

S l o w   up steps
   s l o w   back down
      s l o w l y   sideways
         s l o w l y   around.

Loris Lesynski

Word Box

start
stream
strong
stage
strange
stamp
stepping
stew
story
street

Creating Your Word List

Say these words:

start   stage   stepping   strange   stream

Listen to the beginning blend in each word. Two words –
strange and **stream** – have 3 beginning consonants. When
you say these words, you hear each consonant. We call
these **3-consonant blends**.

1. Make a list of **st** and **str** words you know.

2. With your teacher, list the words you will be learning to spell. You can use: the Word Box, the chant, your own words. These are your Lesson Words.

3. **In your notebook**
   - Write your Lesson Words.
   - Say each word and underline the **st** and **str** blend.

Strategy Spot

Say Your Words S...l...o...w...l...y

If you have trouble spelling a word, say it slowly. This makes it easier to hear each letter in a word. Slowly, say each of your Lesson Words to yourself. Listen for each letter sound. For extra help, ask a friend to say the word.

Zoom in on Your Words

1. **S...t...r...e...a...m** Choose 5 words you need to practise. Use the Strategy Spot to practise them.

2. **Make Your Own Chant** Work with a partner. Read the chant on page 24. Change action words like **stomp** and **tiptoe**. Present your chant to another pair of students.

3. **Make a Word Pyramid** Pick a word you want to practise. Draw a triangle in your notebook. On the first line, print the first letter of the word. On the second line, print the first 2 letters. Continue until you have written all the letters in the word. See a Word Pyramid on page 62, Lesson 15.

4. Missing Words Find words from the Word Box that fit each group. Write the words in your notebook.

a) _ _ _ _ _ and finish **b)** _ _ _ _ _ _ _ _ , stomping, jumping

c) river, lake, _ _ _ _ _ _ **d)** poem, song, _ _ _ _ _

5. Cut, Copy, Spell Follow the directions to do this activity.

1. Cut out 3 cards (6 cm x 12 cm).
2. Choose 3 Lesson Words.
3. Write the Lesson Words on the cards (1 word per card).
4. Trade cards with a partner. Put them face down on a table.
5. Pick up 1 card for your partner to see and say the word.
6. Cover the word. Ask your partner to spell it aloud.
7. Check your partner's spelling.
8. Repeat Steps 5 to 7 with the 2 other words.

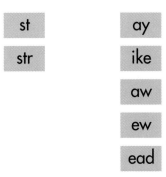

6. St-ay Str-ay Match the **st** and **str** blends to these patterns. If you are not sure that the word is correct, ask a partner to check it. List words you made. Were any of these words your Lesson Words?

st	ay
str	ike
	aw
	ew
	ead

Try This! Find another pattern that makes a word with **st** and **str**.

7. Strange Things Think about 5 things you think are strange. Write a sentence about each one.

FOCUS ON LANGUAGE ▷ Dictionaries

> **dictionary** (dĭc′ shə-nĕr′ ē) *n.* a book that lists words in alphabetical order and explains the meaning of each word. *pl.* **dictionaries**.

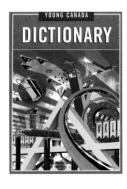

Dictionaries help writers in many ways. We use dictionaries to:

- check our spelling,
- learn how to pronounce a word,
- find out the meaning of new words.

Look at a dictionary in your classroom. Words are placed in alphabetical order (A to Z). This makes it easy to find words.

Here is 1 tip to help you find words quickly. Think of your dictionary as having 2 parts – a front part and a back part. Words that begin with letters **A** to **M** are in the front part. Words that begin with letters **N** to **Z** are in the back part.

1. Find 5 words you want to spell. Look them up in the class dictionary. Write the correct spelling for each word in your Personal Dictionary.

2. Challenge a partner to find a word in a dictionary. Take turns. How long does it take your partner to find a word?

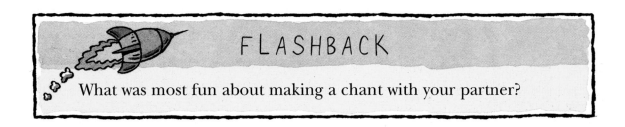

FLASHBACK

What was most fun about making a chant with your partner?

Patterns	Strategies
short vowel sounds bl, cl, fl cr, fr, gr, tr sk, sm, sn, sp st, str	1. Learn about spelling strategies. 2. Say two letters in a blend. 3. Look for blends at the beginning of a word. 4. Make a foldover. 5. Say your words slowly.

Creating Your Word List

In your notebook

- Make a list of 10 words you need to practise.
- Look at the letters you need to focus on.
- Use a coloured pencil to underline these letters. For example:

<u>bl</u>end   <u>str</u>eam

- These are your Review Lesson Words.

Zoom in on Your Words

1. **Be a Slowpoke!** S...l...o...w...l...y say Lesson Words to yourself. Listen to each sound in the words.

2. **Word Pyramids** Pick 1 Lesson Word. Draw a triangle in your notebook. On the first line, print the first letter of the word. On the second line, print the first 2 letters. Continue until you have written all the letters in the word. See a Word Pyramid on page 62, Lesson 15.

3. **Rhyme It** Pick 5 Lesson Words. Write a rhyming word for each (**ground – sound**). Compare each pair of words.

4. **Row and Crow in Crowd** Find and write smaller words in 3 Lesson Words. Ask a partner to find the smaller words.

5. **What's My Word?** Share your Lesson Word list with a partner. Choose 1 word, but do not tell it to your partner. Give your partner up to 3 clues to guess the word. Take turns.

6. **Ways to Sort** Write each Lesson Word on a piece of paper. Sort your words by:
   - pattern (fl**ow**ers, cl**ow**n),
   - sound (**gr**ass, **gr**ound), or
   - meaning (crawl, running).

   Ask a partner to look at your words and tell how you sorted them.

7. **Chant Time** Share Lesson Words with a partner. Together, look at the chant on page 24. Think about words you could use in a chant. Write your chant and try it out. Make any changes, then present your chant to another pair of students.

8. **Make a Mark** Make a bookmark to keep your place in your spelling book. Decorate it with Lesson Words or any words you like.

9. **Make a Foldover** Choose 3 Lesson Words you still need to practise. Use the Strategy Spot on page 21 to learn the words.

FLASHBACK

Which Lesson Words can you now spell? How can you use what you have learned to help you spell other words?

Read this article from a newspaper.

Ape artist escapes from zoo

CAPE TAIL (CP) — An eight-year-old ape escaped from her cage at Cape Tail Zoo yesterday. Zoo keepers say Gail is a gentle gorilla who is also a great painter. "We think she may try to make her way to the lake for a holiday," reports zoo keeper Abe Smith. "She was very tired after her last art display." He has asked the public for help. "If you see a large ape carrying paints and paintbrushes, please call us at 555-SEE-GAIL."

What would you do if you met Gail?

Creating Your Word List

Say these words:

Listen for the **long a** sound in each word. To hear the difference between a **long a** and a **short a**, say **afraid** again. The first **a** is short, the second **a** is long.

1. Read the article, "Ape artist escapes from zoo." List all the **long a** words in a chart like this one.

a-consonant-silent e	ai	ay	other

Word Box

grade
paint
cage
pail
age
tail
chain
play
spray
afraid

2. With your teacher, list the words you will be learning to spell. You can use: the Word Box, the newspaper article, your own words. These are your Lesson Words. Add these challenge words to your list:

beautiful, guess, people

Challenge words are words that can be hard to spell.

3. **In your notebook**
   - Write your Lesson Words.
   - Say the words. Listen to the **long a** sound.
   - Look at the pattern that makes the **long a** sound (**a-consonant-silent e, ai, ay, other**).
   - Circle the **long a** pattern in each word.
   - Add words to your Personal Dictionary. This will help you in your reading and writing.

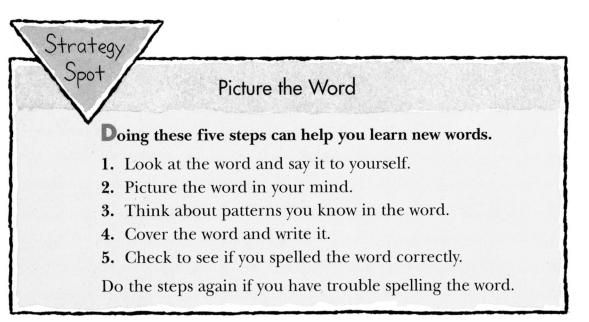

Strategy Spot

Picture the Word

Doing these five steps can help you learn new words.

1. Look at the word and say it to yourself.
2. Picture the word in your mind.
3. Think about patterns you know in the word.
4. Cover the word and write it.
5. Check to see if you spelled the word correctly.

Do the steps again if you have trouble spelling the word.

Zoom in on Your Words

1. **Picture the Words** Choose 3 Lesson Words. Use the Strategy Spot steps to spell them. Remember, most **long a** sounds are made by these patterns: **a-consonant-silent e** (f**a**c**e**), **ai** (p**ai**l), and **ay** (st**ay**).

2. Long a Search Read 1 page from a book or novel. Write the **long a** words you find in your notebook.

Did You Know? Dictionaries tell us which vowels are long. In a dictionary, **tape** will look like this – tāp. The bar above **a** tells us it is long. The missing **e** tells us that it is silent.

3. Missing Person Poster Imagine that you have to make a missing person poster for Gail. What information would you include? Read the article, "Ape artist escapes from zoo" to help you. Make a draft of your poster. Check your spelling before you make your final copy.

4. Then I Heard... Work with a partner. Pick 1 Lesson Word and use it in a sentence. For example, "I wanted to **paint** my door." Your partner must use your **long a** word and 1 of his or her Lesson Words. "You wanted to **paint** your door, but you went to **play**." Keep going until you cannot continue the sentence.

5. Sentence Starters Finish these sentences in your notebook.
a) I played until ...   b) The cat's tail ...   c) The paint was ...

6. Your Local News Count the sections in your local newspaper. Write their titles. Cut out 1 article from 1 section. Bring it to school to share with your classmates.

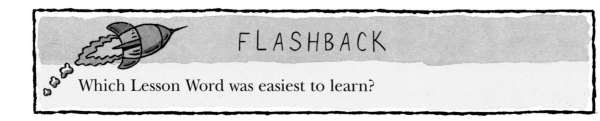

FLASHBACK

Which Lesson Word was easiest to learn?

MEDIA LITERACY

Newspapers

Newspapers give news about where we live – our town or city, province, country, and the rest of the world. We can read about

- people,
- business,
- government,
- sports,
- entertainment.

Newspapers also contain other types of information like

- advertisements,
- letters to the editor,
- birth and death notices.

Look at the newspapers your teacher has collected. Find the news, sports, and entertainment sections in 1 newspaper.

1. With a partner, look at articles in each section. Are they the same length, or are some longer? Talk about reasons for these differences.

2. Next, look at headlines. Why are they important? What headline gets your attention? Tell your partner why.

3. On your own, read 1 article. Draw a picture that will tell others what it is about. Include 3 or 4 words that you like from the article.

Read this poem. Can you imagine living in a tree house?

Tree House

A tree house, a free house,
A secret you and me house,
A high up in the leafy branches
Cozy as can be house.

A street house, a neat house,
Be sure to wipe your feet house
Is not my kind of house at all –
Let's go live in a tree house.

Shel Silverstein

Word Box

team

money

teacher

sleepy

week

please

even

knees

steam

leaf

Creating Your Word List

Say these words:

knees   please   sleepy   even   leaf

Listen for the same sound in each word. Can you hear the **long e** sound? To hear the difference between a **short e** and a **long e**, say **weekend** again. The first **e** is long, the second **e** is short.

1. Make a list of words that have a **long e** sound. You can use the poem to get you started. List your words in a chart like the one on the next page.

ee	ea	e	y	other

2. With your teacher, list the words you will be learning to spell. You can use: the Word Box, the poem, your own words. These are your Lesson Words.

3. **In your notebook**
   - Write your Lesson Words.
   - Say the words. Listen to the **long e** sound.
   - Look at the pattern that makes the **long e** sound (**ee**, **ea**, **e**, **y**, **other**).
   - Circle the **long e** pattern in each word.

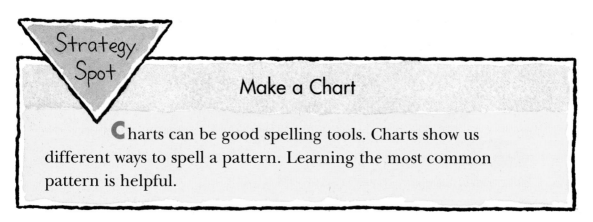

Strategy Spot

Make a Chart

Charts can be good spelling tools. Charts show us different ways to spell a pattern. Learning the most common pattern is helpful.

Zoom in on Your Words

1. **Chart Your Words** Add your Lesson Words to the chart you made at the beginning of this lesson.

2. **Tree House? Street House?** With a partner, list the pros (good things) and cons (bad things) about living in
   a) a tree house   **b)** a regular house or apartment

   Where would you choose to live?

3. **Word Chain** Work with a partner. Take turns writing Lesson Words and words from your Personal Dictionary to make a word chain.

knees steam money

4. **See – Sea** Homophones are words that sound the same, but are spelled differently and have different meanings.

The **sea** was rough.   She wanted to **steal** third base.
I **see** a rainbow.   The ruler was made of **steel**.

Draw a picture of each homophone to show its meaning. Look for more homophones. Add the words to your class list of homophones.

Try This! Write a sentence that includes both homophones. For example: *I wish my **heel** would **heal**.*

5. **Please or Plēz** Dictionaries show long vowels with a bar (-). Look up 1 Lesson Word. See how the dictionary gives the regular spelling, then a spelling that shows how the word is said (pronounced). Write how your Lesson Word is pronounced. Do the same for 2 more words.

Many words that end with a **long e** sound have **y** as the last letter. In words like this – **hurry** – the **y** works as a vowel.

6. **Your Home** Draw the front of your house or apartment. Write 5 words that describe your home.

QUICK TIP

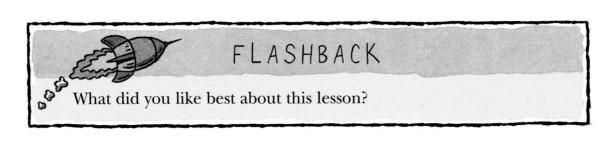

FLASHBACK

What did you like best about this lesson?

36

LITERATURE

Writing Ideas

Shel Silverstein is a famous poet who writes about many things. Reread the poem on page 34. Would you write a poem about where you live? Shel Silverstein must have thought about his house before he wrote "Tree House."

Like famous authors, you can get writing ideas from your own life. Think about what you hear, see, and read each day. What would you like to learn more about?

1. Carry a small notebook for 1 week. Each time you find something interesting, write a few words or sentences about it, or draw a picture.

2. Write 1 or 2 lines of a conversation you heard or were a part of.

3. Think about books you have read. What events were most exciting? Describe them in 1 or 2 lines in your notebook.

4. List each event in your life for 1 day.

5. The next time you can't think of something to write about, pull out your notebook. Find 1 or 2 things and begin to write! Good luck.

Long i

Read these lines from the poem, "Shiny." What words help you to see the moon?

Shiny

But the round full moon,
So clear and white
How brightly she shines
On a winter night!
Slowly she rises,
Higher and higher,
With a cold clear light,
Like ice on fire.

James Reeves

Word Box

mine
price
write
right
high
child
climb
kind
inside
lies

Creating Your Word List

Say these words:

mine   high   lies   child   inside

Listen for the same sound in each word. Can you hear the **long i** sound? To hear the difference between a **long i** and a **short i**, say **inside** again. The first **i** is short, the second **i** is long.

1. Make a list of words that have a **long i** sound. Use words from the poem to get you started. List your words in a chart like the one on the next page.

i-consonant-silent e	igh	ild, imd, ind	other

2. With your teacher, list the words you will be learning to spell. You can use the Word Box, the poem, your own words. These are your Lesson Words.

3. **In your notebook**
   - Write your Lesson Words.
   - Say the words. Listen to the **long i** sound.
   - Look at the pattern that makes the **long i** sound (**i-consonant-silent e**, **igh**, **ild**, **imd**, **ind**, **other**).
   - Add words to your Personal Dictionary. This will help you in your reading and writing.

Strategy Spot

Learn Words by Finger Writing

You can use your finger as a pen when you study your Lesson Words. Trace the letters of a word you are learning on your arm or hand, or on something smooth like your desk. As you trace each letter, say it to yourself. Writing letters with your finger as you say them can help you to remember how to spell a word.

Zoom in on Your Words

1. Use a Strategy Use the Strategy Spot to spell your Lesson Words.

2. **Say (Sā) the Long i** These words are spelled as they are said. Do you know the words? If you have trouble, say each word aloud.

tīd   hī   bī   dī

Try This! Look up 3 Lesson Words in the dictionary. Write how they are said. Give them to a partner. Can your partner say your words?

3. **Look at Your Writing** Choose 1 of your published stories. Read it and underline in pencil **long i** words. How many words did you find?

4. **Making Words** Work with a partner. Write each consonant or blend on a small piece of paper. Write **long i** patterns on same-sized pieces of paper.

Consonant/Blend		Long i Patterns
b	d	ine
m	r	ive
p	t	ime
sm	cr	ide
h	sp	ile

> You may have seen how **y** can act as a vowel to make a **long e** sound (see pg. 34). **Y** can also make a **long i** sound in words like **cry** and **try**.

QUICK TIP

Match each consonant or blend with a **long i** pattern. Write each word you make. Which consonant or blend made the most words? Which pattern made the most words? With your teacher, make a class list of **long i** words.

5. **Tin Foil and More** James Reeves describes the moon as shiny. Make a list of shiny things at home. Ask a family member to make a list of shiny things.

FOCUS ON LANGUAGE ▷ Descriptive Writing

When you read "Shiny" by James Reeves, you "see" the moon in your mind. Find the words the poet used to describe the moon. Write them in your notebook.

Find the words he used to tell us how the moon moved and how it shone. Write them in your notebook, then follow these steps.

1. Pick an object that moves (car, plane, boat).

2. Write words to describe the object – how it looks and how it moves.

3. Read your list of words to a partner.

4. Ask your partner to guess the object you described.

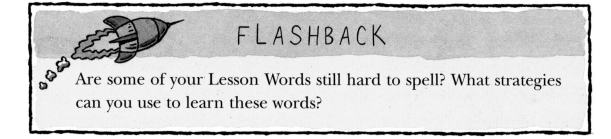

FLASHBACK

Are some of your Lesson Words still hard to spell? What strategies can you use to learn these words?

Imagine that you had to shop for a pet cat or dog. What would you buy at this store?

Word Box

hope
golden
comb
only
clothes
soap
follow
also
rode
almost

Creating Your Word List

Say these words:

Listen for the same sound in each word. Can you hear the **long o** sound? To hear the difference between a **long o** and a **short o**, say **follow**. The first **o** is short. The second **o** is long.

1. Make a list of words that have a **long o** sound. Use words from the pet store picture to get started. List your words in a chart like the one on the next page.

o-consonant-silent e	old, olt, ost	o, ow	other

2. With your teacher, list the words you will be learning to spell. You can use the Word Box, the picture, your own words. These are your Lesson Words.

3. **In your notebook**
   - Write your Lesson Words.
   - Say the words. Listen to the **long o** sound.
   - Look at the pattern that makes the **long o** sound (**o-consonant-silent e**, **old**, **olt**, **ost**, **o**, **ow**, **other**).
   - Circle the **long o** pattern in each word.

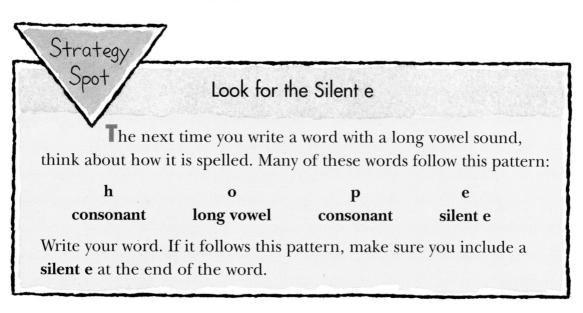

Strategy Spot

Look for the Silent e

The next time you write a word with a long vowel sound, think about how it is spelled. Many of these words follow this pattern:

h	**o**	**p**	**e**
consonant	long vowel	consonant	silent e

Write your word. If it follows this pattern, make sure you include a **silent e** at the end of the word.

Zoom in on Your Words

1. **Write and Sort** Write each Lesson Word on a piece of paper. Think of ways to sort your words. For example, you could sort your words by pattern, meaning, or sound.

2. Get in Shape In your notebook, match these wordprints with the Word Box words that fit them.

a)

b)

c)

3. _ n _ _ balls for Sale! Use these words to complete this ad – only, snow, over, those. Write them in order in your notebook.

4. Make Words with o Patterns Copy this chart in your notebook. Match each consonant with **o patterns** to make words.

Consonants	o Patterns
c	ome
d	
h	one
l	
s	ove

5. For Sale Cut out an interesting advertisement from the newspaper. Talk about the words used in the advertisement with someone at home.

FLASHBACK

What was your favourite spelling activity in this lesson?

Money Words

Look at the advertisements in Toby's Pet Store window(page 42).
Notice that for each product a price is shown in numbers.

1. Write the words that match these signs: ¢ and $.

2. Write, in words, what these coins are worth.

3. Write, in words, what these bills are worth.

4. Write the pet store products in order, from least expensive to most
expensive.

Read these clues. Can you guess the mystery object?

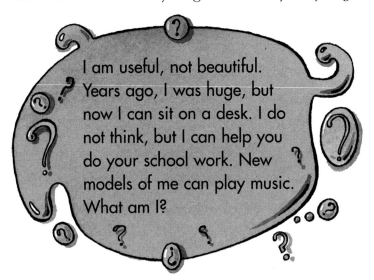

I am useful, not beautiful. Years ago, I was huge, but now I can sit on a desk. I do not think, but I can help you do your school work. New models of me can play music. What am I?

Word Box

new
huge
June
shoes
music
blue
rule
grew
use
true

Creating Your Word List

Say these words:

huge
grew
rule
blue
use

Listen to the **long u** sound in each of these words. You can say the **long u** sound in 2 ways: **yu** (*huge*) and **oo** (*rule*).

1. Make a list of words that have a **long u** sound. You can use the mystery description to get you started. List your words in a chart like this one.

u-consonant-silent e	ew	ue	other

2. With your teacher, list the words you will be learning to spell. You can use: the Word Box, the description, your own words. These are your Lesson Words.

3. In your notebook
- Write your Lesson Words.
- Say the words. Listen to the **long u** sound.
- Look at the pattern that makes the **long u** sound (**u-consonant-silent e**, **ew**, **ue**, **other**).
- Circle the **long u** pattern in each word.
- Add words to your Personal Dictionary. This will help you in your reading and writing.

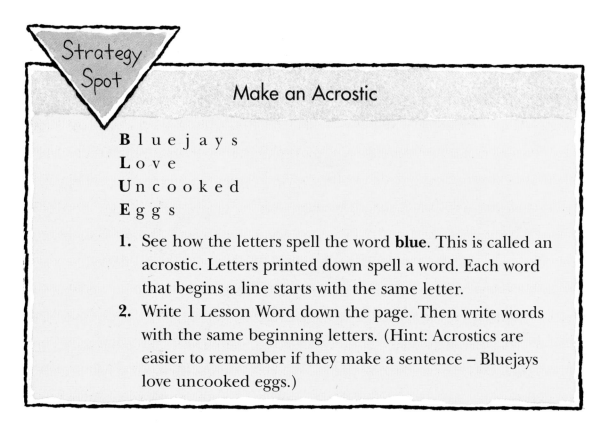

Strategy Spot

Make an Acrostic

B l u e j a y s
L o v e
U n c o o k e d
E g g s

1. See how the letters spell the word **blue**. This is called an acrostic. Letters printed down spell a word. Each word that begins a line starts with the same letter.
2. Write 1 Lesson Word down the page. Then write words with the same beginning letters. (Hint: Acrostics are easier to remember if they make a sentence – Bluejays love uncooked eggs.)

Zoom in on Your Words

1. Acrostics Make an acrostic for a Lesson Word you need to practise.

2. **Homophone Hunt** Find 2 Word Box words that have a homophone partner. Write a sentence or draw a picture that includes them. Add the words to your class list of homophones.

3. **Bumblebee** Play the Bumblebee game with a partner. Choose 1 Lesson Word. Write down a dash (_) for each letter in the word. Your partner has to figure out your word by guessing 1 letter at a time. Only 1 guess of the final word is allowed. For every guess that is not right, draw another part of the Bumblebee.

4. **Word Stairs** Print 1 Lesson Word. Ask a partner to print 1 of his or her Lesson Words that begins with the same letter as the last letter in your word. When you run out of Lesson Words, use other words you know.

```
s u i t
        r
        u
        e
```

5. **What's My Object?** Choose an object, but do not tell it to your partner. Give your partner up to 3 clues to guess the object. Take turns.

6. **Silent e** **Silent e** can make short vowels long. Copy these rows in your notebook. Add an **e** to each **short u** word. Match it to its meaning.

tub	very large
hug	attractive
cut	a thin pipe

7. **Name Acrostics** Make an acrostic for your name or the name of a family member.

FOCUS ON LANGUAGE ▷ Types of Sentences

We use 3 main kinds of sentences when we write. They are:

- a statement   It is a new computer.
- a question   How old is the computer?
- an exclamation   What a computer!

Please look at your writing. Notice what kinds of sentences you use. When do you use exclamation sentences? When do you use questions? Talk with a partner about why using all 3 kinds of sentences could help your writing.

1. Pick 1 sentence from this page. Write it in 2 other ways. Here is 1 example.

- **a)** Look at your writing. (statement)
- **b)** Will you look at your writing? (question)
- **c)** Look at your writing! (exclamation)

What is different about sentences **a** and **c**? The words are the same, but the punctuation is different. Exclamation sentences end with an exclamation mark. This mark shows the reader how to read the sentence. Question marks always end sentences that ask a question.

2. Read the computer description on page 46. Pick an object in the classroom. Write sentences that give clues about the object. Trade your description with a partner. Can your partner identify the object?

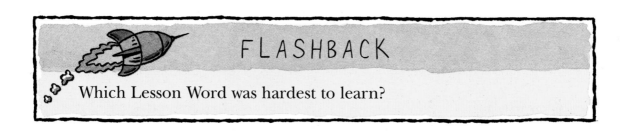

FLASHBACK

Which Lesson Word was hardest to learn?

Patterns	Strategies
long a long e long i long o long u	1. Picture the word. 2. Make a chart. 3. Learn words by finger writing. 4. Look for the silent e. 5. Make an acrostic.

Creating Your Word List

In your notebook
- Make a list of 10 words you need to practise.
- Look at the letters you need to focus on.
- Use a coloured pencil to underline these letters. For example:

pail   lies

- These are your Review Lesson Words.

Zoom in on Your Words

1. **Be a Slowpoke!** S...l...o...w...l...y say Lesson Words to yourself. Listen to each sound in the words.

2. **I See the Sea** Homophones are words that sound the same, but have different meanings and spellings (**tail – tale, week – weak**). Look for homophones in your Lesson Word list or on the class list of homophones. Pick 1 pair of homophones. Draw a picture of each homophone to show its meaning.

3. **Where's the Vowel?** Pick 5 Lesson Words. Write the consonants. Leave a dash (_) for each vowel. For example, **music** would be m _ s _ c. Go back and fill in the missing vowels.

4. **Writing Sounds** Some words in these sentences are written with the dictionary code for long vowel sounds. Write the regular spelling in your notebook.

   a) My shūs got wet in the snō.

   b) I mād a cāk for mī sister's birthdā.

   c) Can you sē the sē from that hī hill?

5. **Word Association** Say 1 Lesson Word. Your partner says a word that your word made him or her think of. Continue for 30 seconds. What were your first and last words?

6. **Word Stairs** Word Stairs are like Word Chains except that they go across and down. Print 1 Lesson Word. Ask a partner to print 1 of his or her words that begins with the same letter as the last letter in your word. When you run out of Lesson Words, use other words you know.

7. **Picture the Word** Choose 3 Lesson Words you still need to practise. Use the Strategy Spot on page 31 to learn the words.

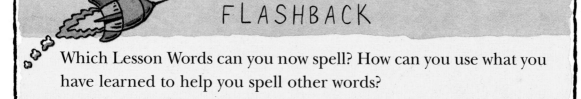

FLASHBACK

Which Lesson Words can you now spell? How can you use what you have learned to help you spell other words?

Read this poem. What other weather words do you know?

Weather

Weather is the sun
Weather is a cloud
Weather is thunder
That shouts out loud

Weather is the wind
Weather is snow
Weather is rain
That helps things grow

Carl Amman

Word Box

their
throw
another
third
mouth
everything
these
earth
anything
those

Creating Your Word List

Say these words:

Which 2 letters are the same in all the words? Where can you find them?

1. Make a list of **th** words you know. Use the poem to get you started. List your words in a chart like this one.

th - (beginning)	- th - (middle)	- th (end)

2. With your teacher, list the words you will be learning to spell. You can use: the Word Box, the poem, your own words. These are your Lesson Words.

3. **In your notebook**
- Write your Lesson Words.
- Circle **th** in each word.
- Underline parts of a word that might be hard for you to spell.

Strategy Spot

Say It Right

Saying a word correctly helps you spell it correctly. Say a word you want to spell. Listen to the letters you hear. Now write the word.

Zoom in on Your Words

1. **Say It Right** Use the Strategy Spot to spell your Lesson Words. Say each word, then spell it in your notebook.

2. **Bases Loaded** Use Word Box words to complete this story. Write them in your notebook.

It was the _ _ ird inning and bases were loaded. Sam was on the pitcher's mound. His team was losing 3 - 0. If they lost this game, they would be out of the series. It was still early, Sam thought, and _ _ _ th _ _ _ was possible. He got ready to th _ _ _ his best pitch. Strike out. He threw _ _ _ th _ _. No one could stop th _ _ _ pitches. Suddenly, _ _ _ _ _ th _ _ _ was quiet. Slugger Gauthier stepped up to bat and dug his toes into the soft _ _ _ th. Sam moaned. Not this, not now!

3. **Find the Missing Word** In your notebook, write the Word Box word that completes each group.

a) air, water, _ _ _ _ _

b) his, her, _ _ _ _ _

c) first, second, _ _ _ _ _

d) this, that, _ _ _ _ _ , _ _ _ _ _

e) nothing, something, _ _ _ _ _ _ _ _ _

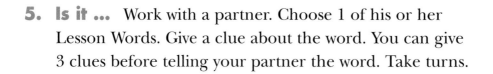

4. **Get in Shape** Choose 5 Lesson Words. Draw the wordprint shapes for them in your notebook. Write the letters for each word.

5. **Is it ...** Work with a partner. Choose 1 of his or her Lesson Words. Give a clue about the word. You can give 3 clues before telling your partner the word. Take turns.

6. **Pairs of Pears** **Their** has a homophone partner – **there**. Write the partners in your notebook. Add them to your class list of homophones.

7. **Magic Letter Box** Work with a partner. See how many **th** words you can make using these letters.

t	r	a
s	th	p
i	e	n

 Did You Know?

The word **the** is one of the most used words in the English language. Other words that are used often are **a** and **and**.

8. **Weather is...** Read the weather poem on page 52. See how most lines start with *Weather is...* . Use this as a model to write your own poem. You could use these starters:

school is ...   friends are ...   pets are ...

54

FOCUS ON LANGUAGE Compound Words

A compound word is 2 smaller words that have been combined to make 1 word. It has the same meaning as the 2 words it contains.

down + stairs = downstairs
up   + stairs = upstairs

1. Find the 2 compound words in the Word Box. Tell a partner what you think each word means.

2. Write these words in your notebook. Draw a line from **A** to **B** to make compound words. One has been done for you.

A	**B**
some	selves
shell	work
play	boat
our	fish
life	where
home	ground

3. Pick 1 compound word from #2. Draw a picture of the word.

4. Choose 1 of these words: **over**, **under**, or **some**. With a partner, list compound words that begin with this word.

5. Invent a new compound word. Draw a picture of each word. Can a partner guess your new word? See the example "superlunch."

supxer

FLASHBACK

Why can compound words be easy to spell?

55

Find the question words – **who**, **what**, **when**, **where**, **why**, **how**. Newspaper writers answer these questions every day.

Word Box

which
who
white
where
when
what
wheel
whose
while
why

Creating Your Word List

Say these words:

What sounds do you hear when you say **wh** words? Ask a partner to say the words aloud. Listen to the different sounds **wh** can make.

1. Make a list of **wh** words you know. Use the newsroom picture to get you started.

2. With your teacher, list the words you will be learning to spell. You can use: the Word Box, the picture, your own words. These are your Lesson Words.

3. In your notebook

- Write your Lesson Words.
- Circle **wh** in each word.
- Underline parts of a word that might be hard for you to spell.
- Add **wh** words to your Personal Dictionary. This can help you in your reading and writing.

Strategy Spot

Look, Say, Cover, Write, Check

Here is another 5-step strategy to help you learn how to spell new words.

1. Look at a Lesson Word.
2. Say the word slowly to yourself.
3. Cover the word with a piece of paper.
4. Write how you think the word is spelled.
5. Uncover the word to check your spelling.

If you have trouble spelling the word, try the strategy again.

Zoom in on Your Words

1. **The Five-Step Strategy** Pick 5 Lesson Words you need to practise. Use the Strategy Spot to help you learn how to spell them.

2. **Scrambled Words** Some of the Word Box words have been scrambled. Can you unscramble them?
   a) hilew   **b)** owseh   **c)** twieh   **d)** hewel

Try This! Scramble some of your Lesson Words. Ask a partner to put them in order.

Look for **wh** at the beginning of a word, not in the middle or at the end.

QUICK TIP

3. Shush! We're Playing Concentration

Cut a sheet of paper into 20 equal-sized squares. Write your Lesson Words twice – 1 word per square. Turn the squares over, and then mix them up. Number the **back** of the squares from 1 to 20. Lay the squares down so that the numbers are showing. Take turns turning over any 2 numbers until you get a pair of matching words.

4. Question a Story

Read to a partner a story you are writing. Your partner asks you who, what, when, where, and why questions about the story. Include missing information in your story.

5. What?

Say the word **what**. A partner says it another way. Take turns, but change your voice each time you say the word. Use your voice to show you are mad, happy, pleased, nervous, shy, confident, excited.

6. A Day in the Life of...

Make a chart like this one. Write 10 things you did today. Ask a family member to do the same.

What	Where	When
got out of bed	at home	at 8:00 a.m.

Trade pages. Did you write about some of the same activities?

FLASHBACK

Why is the Strategy Spot helpful?

FOCUS ON LANGUAGE ▷ Contractions

When we speak and write, we often combine 2 words. These are called contractions. Here are 3 examples:

a) **What is** the book called?   **What's** the book called?
b) **I am** going to the library.   **I'm** going to the library.
c) We **did not** leave.   We **didn't** leave.

a) **What is** becomes **What's**. The apostrophe (') takes the place of the letter **i** in **is**.

b) **I am** becomes **I'm**. The apostrophe (') takes the place of the letter **a** in **am**.

c) **did not** becomes **didn't**. The apostrophe (') takes the place of the letter **o** in **not**.

1. Look through newspapers and magazines. Copy 10 contractions. (Hint: Look for apostrophes.) Write each contraction in your notebook, then write the 2 words that make it up.

2. Listen to people speak. In your notebook, write 5 contractions that you hear and the words that make them up.

3. Start a class list of contractions. Share your list with 3 or 4 other students.

Long ago, the words **of the clock** were used when telling time. *It is 8 of the clock.* Then it was shortened to **o'clock**. The apostrophe takes the place of the letter **f** and the word **the**.

Say these tongue twisters quickly 3 times.

Sheldon sharpened his shortest scissors.

Shelagh's silver shoes were on a shelf in the shed.

She sells seashells on sandy seashores.

Word Box

share
dishes
finish
shadow
shiver
mushroom
brush
shouldn't
wishful
smash

Creating Your Word List

Say these words:

shadow
share
wishful
dishes
smash

What sound is the same in all 5 words? Write the letters that make the sound. Notice how **s** and **h** come together to make the sound we hear in **shoes**.

1. Make a list of **sh** words you know. You can use the tongue twisters to get started. List your words in a chart like this one.

sh - (beginning)	- sh - (middle)	- sh (end)

2. With your teacher, list the words you will be learning to spell. You can use: the Word Box, the tongue twisters, your own words. These are your Lesson Words.

3. **In your notebook**
   - Write your Lesson Words.
   - Circle **sh** in each word.
   - Underline parts of a word that might be hard for you to spell.

Strategy Spot

Make a Rhyming Word

When you are not sure how to spell a word, think of a word you know that rhymes. Write the word you know, then write the word you want to spell.

Zoom in on Your Words

1. **Care - Share** Write rhyming words for 3 Lesson Words.

2. **Words in Words** Look for smaller words in your Lesson Words (dishes – is, dish, she, he).

3. **Word Association** Work with a partner. Choose 1 Lesson Word. Your partner says a word your Lesson Word makes him or her think of. You say a word your partner's word makes you think of. Do this for 30 seconds. How many words can you say?

4. **Scrunched-up Words** Find 3 Word Box words that have been scrunched up. Write them in your notebook.

sharemushroomshouldn't

5. Tongue Twister Time Use your Lesson Words to write a tongue twister. Include as many words as you can that have the same beginning sound. Share your tongue twister with a partner.

6. Word Pyramid Pick 1 Lesson Word you want to practise. Draw a triangle in your notebook. On the first line, print the first letter of the word. On the second line, print the first 2 letters. Continue until you have written all the letters in the word.

Sh is like **th**. It can be found at the beginning, middle, or end of a word.

s
sh
sha
shar
share

QUICK TIP

7. Round the Word Trip Choose 1 Lesson Word. Make boxes like these. Write your Lesson Word in the first box. In the next box, write a word it makes you think of. Continue until you have filled the boxes. Where did your trip end?

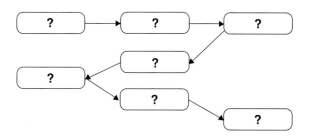

? → ? → ?

?

?

?

?

8. Home Practice Use the rhyming word strategy to spell your words at home.

FOCUS ON LANGUAGE ▷ Naming Words (Nouns)

A noun is a word that names a person, an animal, a place, or a thing. Often, a noun will have **a**, **an**, or **the** in front of it. A noun has a capital letter when it names a particular person (**S**ue, **M**rs. **S**mith) or place (**R**ideau **C**anal, **O**ttawa, **R**iverside **D**rive).

1. Put **the** in front of each word. If the word is not a noun, it will not make sense.

children	did	club	puppy
tell	have	clock	class
pencil	nickel	there	teach

2. Read these sentences. Write the nouns in your notebook.
   a) The dentist checked her teeth. **b)** Do kittens eat bananas?
   c) My sister is my best friend. **d)** The clock was broken.

3. Read the tongue twisters at the top of page 60. Write the nouns in your notebook.

4. Write your name and address. Underline the nouns.

5. Work with a partner. In 2 minutes, write all the nouns you can see in the classroom. Trade lists with another pair of students. Did you list the same nouns?

FLASHBACK

How can you help a partner spell a word?

Would this ad make you want to eat Peach 'n Cherry Chow?

Word Box

match
catch
cheese
chicken
chair
choice
coach
scratch
chalk
children

Creating Your Word List

Say these words:

cheese   chalk   chair   children   scratch

What sound is the same in all 5 words? Write the letters that make the sound. Notice how **c** and **h** come together to make the sound we hear in **children**.

1. Make a list of **ch** words you know. Use the advertisement to get started. List your words in a chart like this one.

ch - (beginning)	- ch - (middle)	- ch (end)

2. With your teacher, list the words you will be learning to spell. You can use: the Word Box, the advertisement, your own words. These are your Lesson Words.

3. **In your notebook**
   - Write your Lesson Words.
   - Circle **ch** in each word.
   - Underline parts of a word that might be hard for you to spell.
   - Add **ch** words to your Personal Dictionary. This can help you in your reading and writing.

Strategy Spot

Proofreading – Scan Back!

Proofreading is what you do to find spelling and grammar mistakes. A proofreading tip is to read your work backwards. This way you will pay attention to the spelling of each word instead of the meaning of what you have written. To proofread the sentence "The fish swam home," you would read the words in this order: "home swam fish The."

Zoom in on Your Words

1. **Cheese Please!** Look at the Word Box words. For each word, try to find rhyming words. Which word made the most rhymes?

2. **Writer Required** Look at the advertisement at the start of the Lesson. Write an advertisement for your favourite food.

3. **Reader Required** Work with a partner. Imagine that you are taping your ad for radio. How would you read it? Practise with your partner, then present your ad.

4. **Sentence Starters** Finish these sentences in your notebook.
   a) The coach ...   **b)** The children ran ...
   c) Ten chairs ...   **d)** Her choice was ...

5. **Make a Letter Ladder** Pick a Lesson Word. Write it in a row, from top to bottom. Use other Lesson Words to fill in the ladder. You can also use other words you know how to spell.

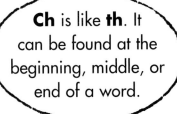

Ch is like **th**. It can be found at the beginning, middle, or end of a word.

QUICK TIP

```
        c  h  a  i  r
     m  a  t  c  h
s  c  r  a  t  c  h
        c  h  a  l  k
     c  h  o  i  c  e
```

6. **Anagrams** An *anagram* is a word where the order of letters has been changed to make another word (**eat – tea**). Write the answers to these **ch** and **sh** anagram puzzles in your notebook.

   a) a fruit that costs very little   _ _ _ _ _   peach
   b) a charm in the third month   _ _ _ _ _   charm
   c) to close small cabins   _ _ _ _   huts

7. **Child Champion Wins Prize** Look through newspapers and magazines for **ch** words. Use 1 or more of your words to write a headline. Bring your headline to class to share with other students.

FOCUS ON LANGUAGE ▷ Syllables

Ask a partner to say **crunch**, then **crunchy**. Notice how your partner says crunch as a 1 part and crunchy as 2 parts. These parts, or beats, are called **syllables**. Every word has at least 1 syllable.

1. Say your Lesson Words aloud. List your words in a chart like this one.

One Part	Two Parts
(crunch)	(crunch y)

2. With a partner, read the advertisement on page 64. For each part, clap your hands. Here is how Juan and his partner would clap the parts.

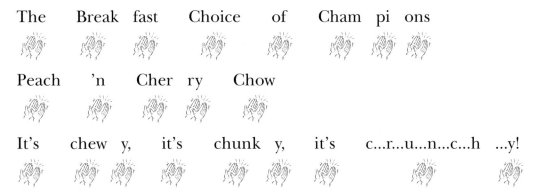

The   Break   fast   Choice   of   Cham   pi   ons

Peach   'n   Cher   ry   Chow

It's   chew   y,   it's   chunk   y,   it's   c...r...u...n...c...h   ...y!

3. Clap each part of a favourite poem or chant. How many syllables are in the first line of the poem?

Did You Know? Dictionaries show us how to say a word by breaking it up in syllables.

FLASHBACK

How does knowing about syllables help you spell?

67

Silent Consonants

Look at and listen to the silent consonants.

Knight Knud Knudsen
Kneeling on his knee
Knocking on a door
Someone is in trouble
Better him than me!

Word Box

know

wrong

light

sight

wrap

wrote

bright

knife

wreck

knight

Creating Your Word List

Say these words:

know

wrong

wrote

bright

knight

Which letters (consonants) do you see but not hear?
We call these **silent consonants**.

1. Make a list of silent consonant words you know. You can use the picture to get you started. List your words in a chart like this one.

kn	wr	gh	other

2. With your teacher, list the words you will be learning to spell. You can use: the Word Box, the picture and poem, your own words. These are your Lesson Words. Add these challenge words to your Lesson Words:

bought, brought

3. **In your notebook**
- Write your Lesson Words.
- Circle the **silent consonants**.
- Underline parts of a word that might be hard for you to spell.

Say the Silent Consonant

Here is a strategy to help you remember silent consonants. Say the silent consonant in a word you are learning to spell. For example, you want to spell **knot**. Say to yourself **k**-*not*. This will remind you that **knot** has a silent **k**.

Zoom in on Your Words

1. **Unsilent Consonants**   Say the silent consonants in each Lesson Word.

2. **Colour Your Words**   Print each Lesson Word on a piece of paper. Make the letters large and leave a space between them. Trace over letters you say using 1 colour. Trace over silent consonants in another colour.

3. **Rhyme Time** Pick 1 Lesson Word. Make a list of words that rhyme with it. Some will have the same silent consonants, others will not. Try other Lesson Words. Which word made the most rhyming words?

4. **Homophone Hunt** Make homophone pairs. Unscramble the silent consonant words in **A** and match them with their partner in **B**. Add them to your class list of homophones.

A	B
oktn	knight
gtinh	new
wonsk	not
pwar	nose
wken	rap

Kn and **wr** are usually at the beginning of a word. They are never at the end. **Gh** is silent when it is followed by **t** at the end of a word (thought).

QUICK TIP

Did You Know? Long ago, there were no silent letters. People said every letter in a word. Think how you would say all the letters in **wreck**.

5. **TV Favourites** Write the names of your top 5 television programs. Put an **X** through the silent letters.

FLASHBACK

Which silent consonant words did you find easiest to spell – words with **wr**, **kn**, or **gh**?

Posters

Have you made a poster for school this year? Liam made this poster to go with a story he wrote about staying on his uncle's farm.

1. Before you begin, think about:
   • what you want your poster to show,
   • how many things you can include,
   • what you will use (torn paper, markers, cut-out pictures).

2. Make a rough outline of your poster. This will tell you if you have too much or too little on your poster.

3. Make a good copy. If you want, label your poster like Liam did. Check the spelling of each word before you write it in pen or marker.

4. Display your poster!

Patterns	Strategies
th wh sh ch silent consonants	1. Say it right. 2. Look, say, cover, write, check. 3. Make a rhyming word. 4. Proofreading – Scan back! 5. Say the silent consonant.

Creating Your Word List

In your notebook

- Make a list of 10 words you need to practise.
- Look at the letters you need to focus on.
- Use a coloured pencil to underline these letters. For example:

<u>wh</u>ich   li<u>gh</u>t

- These are your Review Lesson Words.

Zoom in on Your Words

1. **Be a Slowpoke!** S...l...o...w...l...y say each Lesson Word to yourself. Listen to every sound in the word.

2. **Sha • dow** Choose 3 of your longest Lesson Words. Snap, clap, or tap the syllables. Write each word. Leave a space to show syllables.

3. **Wordprints** Make wordprints for 5 Lesson Words you would like to practise. For each word, draw the shape then write the letters.

4. **Colour Your Words** Print your Lesson Words. Leave a space between each letter. Use a coloured pencil to trace over the letters. Use another colour to trace over difficult letters.

5. **Two Words in One** A compound word is made up of 2 smaller words. Look at your Lesson Words. Are any words compounds? If yes, underline the 2 smaller words that make up the compound.

6. **Name the Nouns** Circle Lesson Words that are nouns.

7. **What's This?** Read these contractions. Write the words that make up each contraction in your notebook.

can't   shouldn't   didn't   they've

8. **A Trip Without Maps** Make boxes like these in your notebook. Write 1 Lesson Word in the first box. In the next box, write the word it makes you think of. Fill all of the boxes. Where did your trip end?

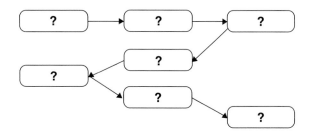

9. **Look, Say, Cover, Write, Check** Choose 3 Lesson Words you still need to practise. Use the strategy on page 57 to learn the words.

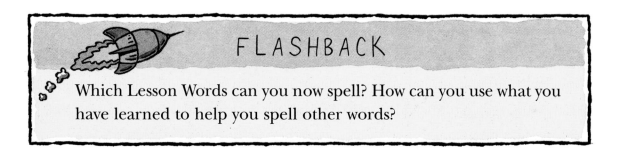

FLASHBACK

Which Lesson Words can you now spell? How can you use what you have learned to help you spell other words?

Decide which sentences are right (true) or wrong (false). Where can you find answers to these questions?

1. Guppies are baby fish.
2. German shepherds are big dogs.
3. A hedgehog is a real animal.
4. There are many giant pandas in the world.
5. An iguana has six legs.

Word Box

dragon
page
large
garden
wagon
together
gentle
giant
began
gather

Creating Your Word List

Say these words:

garden
giant
dragon
began
large

Ask a partner to say the words aloud. Hear the sound of **hard g** in **garden** and **soft g** in **giant**.

1. Make a list of words that have **hard g** and **soft g** sounds. You can use the sentences to get you started. List your words in a chart like this one.

Hard g	Soft g

2. With your teacher, list the words you will be learning to spell. You can use: the Word Box, the sentences, your own words. These are your Lesson Words.

3. In your notebook
- Write your Lesson Words.
- Circle the **hard g** or **soft g** in each word.
- Add words to your Personal Dictionary. This can help you in your reading and writing.

Listen to the Sounds
Some Consonants Make

Some consonants make more than 1 sound. Consonants like **c** (**c**at, **c**ent) and **g** (**g**um, **g**iant) can make both hard and soft sounds. **Soft g**, like **giant**, makes the same sound as **j**. You can't tell these consonants by their sound so you must look at the letters that make up a **c** or **g** word.

Zoom in on Your Words

1. Listen for g Say your Lesson Words. Listen to the sound **g** makes in each word. How many words contain a **hard g**? How many words contain a **soft g**?

2. True or False? Use Lesson Words to make true and false sentences like those on page 74. Trade sentences with a partner. Answer them with a **T** (true) or **F** (false). If you want, look up answers in a magazine or book, or on the computer.

> **Hard g** (game) is usually found before **a**, **o**, or **u**. **Soft g** (gym) is usually found before **e**, **i**, or **y**.

QUICK TIP

3. Scrunched-up Words Find 3 Word Box words that have been scrunched up. Write them in your notebook.

dragongardentogether

Try This! Scrunch 3 Lesson Words. Can a partner say your words?

4. Question–Question Pick 5 Word Box words. For each word, make a clue. A partner guesses the answer and makes it into a question. For example, the word is **garden**. The clue is, "This is a place where flowers grow." The answer is, "What is a garden?" Guess your partner's words.

5. To • geth • er Count the syllables in each Word Box word. Write them in a chart like this. Add your Lesson Words. Check word breaks in a dictionary.

One Syllable	Two Syllables	Three Syllables
page	ga ther	to geth er

6. I Spy Play "I Spy" with a family member. Each person must spy at least 1 thing that is spelled with a **g**.

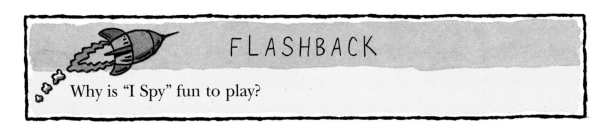

FLASHBACK

Why is "I Spy" fun to play?

Connecting with

MEDIA

Libraries

Did you use books, magazines, or the computer to help you decide if the sentences on page 74 were true or false?

Imagine that you are writing a report on sports. You could get information from:

- the library,
- the Internet,
- CDs,
- books, magazines, and newspapers.

Follow these steps the next time you go to the library.

1. List places where you can find information.

2. Draw a map of the library. Label your drawing.

3. Write tips on using the library (be quiet, use the computer to find books).

What do you think is in the sack?

What's in the Sack?

What's in the sack? What's in the sack?
Is it some mushrooms or is it the moon?
Is it love letters or downy goosefeathers?
Or maybe the world's most enormous balloon?
What's in the sack? That's all they ask me.
Could it be popcorn or marbles or books?
Is it two years' worth of your dirty laundry,
Or the biggest ol' meatball that's ever been cooked?

Shel Silverstein

Word Box

school
stood
wooden
spoon
cookies
tooth
broom
moon
food
wool

Creating Your Word List

Say these words:

Listen to the sounds **oo** can make. Say each word again.
Decide if it makes the **oo** sound of **zoo** or the **oo** sound
of **foot**.

1. Make a list of **oo** words. You can use the poem to get
   started.

2. With your teacher, list the words you will be learning to spell. You can use: the Word Box, the poem, your own words. These are your Lesson Words.

3. In your notebook
- Write your Lesson Words.
- Circle **oo** in each word.

Does It Look Right?

When you are not sure how to spell a word, write it 2 ways. Circle the way that looks right. For example, which word looks right?

wodden   wooden

If you chose **wooden**, you would be right.

Zoom in on Your Words

1. One Word, Two Ways Choose 5 Lesson Words you want to practise. Write each word 2 ways. Give the pairs of words to a partner. Have him or her circle the word that looks right in each pair. Check the words to see if your partner chose correctly.

2. Three of a Kind Read "What's in the Sack?" See how the poet rhymes **oo** words like *moon* and *balloon*. Write 2 other words that rhyme with *moon*.

Try This! Choose 2 Lesson Words. For each, write 2 rhyming words.

3. Print/Spell Write Lesson Words on small pieces of paper. Look at each word and say it slowly. Turn the papers face down on a table. A partner picks up 1 paper and says the word. Spell it to your partner. If you have trouble, your partner puts the word away so that you can practise it later.

4. Clues with oo Trade Lesson Word lists with a partner. Pick 3 of your partner's words and make up a clue for each. Your partner guesses the word, then spells it aloud or writes it on a piece of paper. Check your partner's spelling. If it is right, your partner gives you a clue for a word. If it is wrong, give another clue to your partner.

5. Sentence Starters Finish these sentences in your notebook.

a) At school, ...   **b)** She stood ...

c) Brown wool ...   **d)** My favourite food ...

6. Food Search With a family member, list kitchen and food words that include the **oo** pattern. Bring your list to school and make a class list of **oo** kitchen and food words.

FLASHBACK

How does the Strategy Spot help you?

LITERATURE

List Poems

Here is an example of a list poem. They can be fun to write.

Milk
Cold
White
Food
Bubbles
Froth
Slurp
Oh, that tastes good!

Directions for Writing a List Poem

1. Look over your Lesson Words.

2. Pick 1 word that you like.

3. List all the words your word makes you think of. (You will not use all of them in your poem.)

4. Choose words that best describe your Lesson Word.

5. Organize your words in a list.

6. Add a sentence to complete your poem.

7. Illustrate your poem.

Read these paragraphs from a short story by Carl Amman.

Sarah looked around the house. She went outside and down the hill.

"Hello, Brown Cow," Sarah called out. Brown Cow raised her head at the sound of the girl's voice. Her big round eyes stared at Sarah without interest.

"Is it true you give us chocolate milk?" Sarah asked. Brown Cow flicked her tail and stared. Then she bowed her head to the ground and began to eat and swallow the grass. Sarah thought of how the cow's mouth was like a lawn mower.

"Good bye, Brown Cow. We will talk tomorrow." With that, Sarah turned to follow the path to her house.

Word Box

flowers
count
downstairs
somehow
shout
outside
cloud
clown
town
around

Creating Your Word List

Say these words:

count   flowers   cloud   shout   downstairs

What sound is the same in all the words? What 2 patterns spell the **ow** sound in **cow**?

1. Make a list of **ou** and **ow** words. List your words in a chart like the one on the next page.

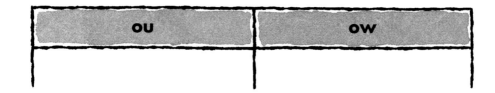

ou	**ow**

2. With your teacher, list the words you will be learning to spell. You can use: the Word Box, the story, your own words. These are your Lesson Words.

3. **In your notebook**
   - Write your Lesson Words.
   - Circle **ou** or **ow** in each word.
   - Add **ou** and **ow** words to your Personal Dictionary. This can help you in your reading and writing.

Strategy Spot

Say and Write

It can be hard to remember how to spell a sound when there is more than 1 spelling pattern for it. One strategy is to say the word, then write it. Say each letter as you write it. Highlight the spelling pattern. This will help you connect the spelling pattern to the rest of the word.

Zoom in on Your Words

1. **Say It, Write It!** Use the Strategy Spot to write your Lesson Words. You can list them under the headings **ou** and **ow**.

2. **Brown Cow** Look at the opener. In your notebook, write **ou** and **ow** words the author used. Highlight words that rhyme.

3. Word Chain Work with a partner. Take turns writing Lesson Words and words from your Personal Dictionary to make a word chain.

downstairs shout to

4. A Pyramid Poem Pick 1 Lesson Word and write it in your notebook. On the next line, write a word it makes you think of. Illustrate or decorate your finished pyramid poem.

count
count slowly
count slowly then
count slowly then count
count slowly then count quickly

Ou is at the beginning of words. **Ow** can be in the middle or at the end of words.

QUICK TIP

5. Bumblebee Play Bumblebee with a partner. Player A chooses a Lesson Word and makes a dash for each letter in the word. Player B figures out the word by guessing 1 letter at a time. Only 1 guess of the final word is allowed. For every incorrect guess, Player A draws another part of the Bumblebee. Switch roles.

6. Making Words Start with the letter or blend on the biggest circle. Add **ou** or **ow** from the second circle. End the word with 1 set of letters from the smallest circle. Write each word you make. How many words did you make?

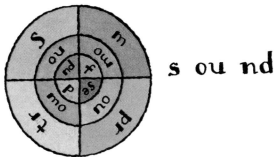

s ou nd

7. Clouds Look up at the sky. Draw what you see in a cloud.

FOCUS ON LANGUAGE ▷ Conversation in Writing

Look at page 82. Notice how the author shows when Sarah speaks. When writers include conversation, they follow 3 main rules:

- put quotation marks (" ") around a speaker's words,
- start a new paragraph for every speaker,
- include punctuation marks (, . ! ?) inside quotation marks.

Look at page 82 to answer the first question.

1. What was the last sentence Sarah said to the cow?

2. Find a conversation you have written. Check that you followed the 3 main rules.

3. Punctuate your dialogue.

4. Trade your writing with a partner. Proofread each other's work.

FLASHBACK

How would you help a partner learn about **ou** and **ow** patterns?

Across

1 straw_____,
    rasp_____
2 sit on this
4 up, down, _____
6 ride this to school
8 _____ to music
10 another word for glue
12 not new

Down

1 game with bases, a bat
3 find this by a lake or sea
5 rises and sets each day
7 also known as pennies
9 large body of water
11 we

Answers to this crossword puzzle contain the **s** sound. Use the clues to find the answers. Write them in your notebook.

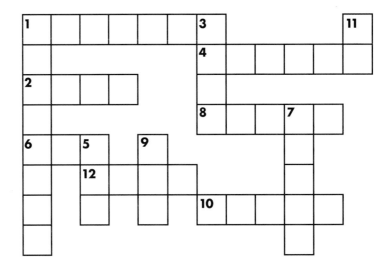

Word Box

nice
baseball
Sunday
prince
cents
across
send
pencil
class
race

Creating Your Word List

Say these words:

send Sunday prince
across cents

What sound is the same in all the words? Write the letters that make this sound.

1. Make a list of words that have the **s** sound. The sound can be spelled **s**, **ss**, **c**. Use the words from the crossword to get you started. List your words in a chart like the one on the next page.

s	ss	c

2. With your teacher, list the words you will be learning to spell. You can use: the Word Box, the crossword, your own words. These are your Lesson Words.

3. **In your notebook**
   - Write your Lesson Words.
   - Circle the **s** sound in each word.

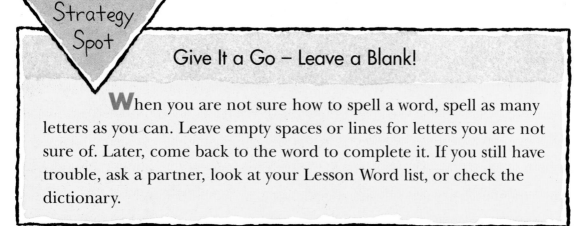

Strategy Spot

Give It a Go – Leave a Blank!

When you are not sure how to spell a word, spell as many letters as you can. Leave empty spaces or lines for letters you are not sure of. Later, come back to the word to complete it. If you still have trouble, ask a partner, look at your Lesson Word list, or check the dictionary.

Zoom in on Your Words

1. **Give It a Go** Use the Strategy Spot to learn your Lesson Words. For each, write letters you know. Leave blanks for letters you are not sure of. Later, come back to your words.

2. **Word Stairs** Print 1 of your Lesson Words. Ask a partner to print 1 of his or her words that begins with the same letter as the last letter in your word. When you run out of words, use other words you know.

3. **Word Pole** Copy this word pole in your notebook. Use the clues to find words from the Word Box. Circle the letters to discover what is "out of this world."

1. day after Saturday
2. _____ and princess
3. summer sport
4. 100 of these make 1 dollar
5. write with this

4. **Rhyme It!** Work with a partner. Pick Lesson Words you need to practise. Together, think of rhyming words for each Lesson Word. Write your words, for example, **race**, **ace**, **space**.

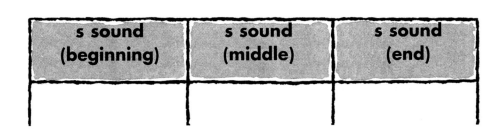

When **c** comes before vowels **e** or **i**, it makes an **s** sound (ice, city, circus).

5. **Prin_ e** Trade Lesson Word lists with a partner. Write the words, but make a dash where the **s** sound is made. Your partner must decide which **s** pattern completes the word.

6. **Classify** Make a chart like this one. Write each word you have met in this lesson under the correct head.

QUICK TIP

s sound (beginning)	s sound (middle)	s sound (end)

7. **Puzzle Page** Look at a newspaper. Many have word puzzles – scrambled words, fill-in-the-blanks – in the family or entertainment section. Complete a puzzle with a family member.

FOCUS ON LANGUAGE Words that Mean the Same – Synonyms

A synonym is a word that has the same or almost the same meaning as another word. A synonym for **glad** is *happy*. A synonym for **fast** is *quick*.

You can find synonyms in dictionaries and thesauruses, and on computer thesauruses. A thesaurus is like a dictionary, but instead of giving definitions it lists other words that share the same meaning.

1. Look at the crossword puzzle on page 86. Find the synonym for **glue** and the synonym for **pennies**.

2. Write these words in your notebook. Draw a line between words that are synonyms. The first 1 has been done for you.

writer	examination
wise	bit
piece	author
lose	smart
test	misplace

3. Many writers use the word **nice** too much. Look in a dictionary or thesaurus for synonyms of nice.

4. Look through your writing. Do you use 1 word too often? Find a synonym for that word. The next time you write it, use the synonym for your old word.

FLASHBACK

How does the Give It a Go strategy help you spell words?

Read this report. Have you read books by this author?

Encyclopedia Brown: Boy Detective

by Donald Sobol

In these books, Encyclopedia Brown is a ten-year-old detective who solves crimes. "Encyclopedia" is his nickname because he knows so many facts about everything. He solves 10 cases in each book. In one case, he discovers who has taken a set of roller skates. At the end of each case, you get to guess how he solved it. The answers are at the back of the book, but please don't look before you finish!

Word Box

monkey
kept
o'clock
carry
cracker
think
could
doctor
snack
colour

Creating Your Word List

Say these words:

carry   kept   colour   think   cracker

What sound is the same in all of these words? Write the letters that make this sound.

1. Make a list of words that have the **k** sound. Use words in the report to get you started. List the words in a chart like the one on the next page.

c	k	ck

2. With your teacher, list the words you will be learning to spell. You can use: the Word Box, the report, your own words. These are your Lesson Words.

3. **In your notebook**
   - Write your Lesson Words.
   - Circle the **k** sound in each word.
   - Add words to your Personal Dictionary. This can help you in your reading and writing.

Strategy Spot

Read Aloud to Proofread

When you proofread, you usually look for misspelled words. Reading your work aloud can help you find other mistakes (punctuation, a word you use too often). As you read, circle mistakes. Complete your reading, then make your changes.

Zoom in on Your Word List

1. **Read Aloud** Look at a piece of your writing. Use the Strategy Spot to find mistakes.

2. **Look for Little Words** Choose 5 Lesson Words you want to practise. Look for a smaller word in each word. Use the smaller word and the Lesson Word in the same sentence. For example: A **car** can **carry** heavy things.

3. **Monkey Alert**   Use Word Box words to complete these sentences. Write the missing words in your notebook.

At eight _ ' _ _ _ _ _ each morning, Petra began work at the pet store. Her favourite animal was a _ _ _ _ _ _ named Theo. Petra went to his cage and looked in. Theo was gone! Petra _ _ _ _ _ not _ _ _ _ _ . Theo's blanket that he liked to _ _ _ _ _ with him was there and so was the _ _ _ _ _ _ _ he _ _ _ _ under his bed. Petra knew she had to tell her boss, _ _ _ _ _ _ Klikinbocker. She also had to tell Encyclopedia Brown. This was a perfect case for him!

4. **The ck Challenge**   With a partner, choose a card from the **A** pile. Match it to cards in the **B** pile. Write words you make. Compare lists with another pair of students. Did you make the same words?

A	B
st	eck
fl	ack
sn	ick
tr	ock
sh	uck

Ck always comes *after* a short vowel sound.

QUICK TIP

5. **K Sound Search**   Write the names of objects in your home that have a **k** sound.

FLASHBACK

What surprised you when you were proofreading?

TECHNOLOGY

Spell Checks

The student who wrote the report on page 90 did it on a computer. Before she published it, she did a spell check. Here is her report before she used the spell check. Can you find the spelling mistakes? (Hint: There are 10 mistakes.)

In these boocs, Encyclopedia Brown is a ten-year-old detecive who solves krimes. "Encyclopedia" is his nicname because he nows so many facts about everything. He solves 10 kases in each book. In one case, he discovers who has takken a set of roller scates. At the end of each case, you get to guess how he solved it. The answers are at the bak of the book, but please don't lok before you finish!

1. The next time you have to write something – a report, a story – do it on the computer.
2. Read your work before you do a spell check. Make your changes.
3. Do a spell check. See how the computer gives you words to choose from. Make your choices.
4. How does a spell check help you learn about spelling?

Patterns	Strategies
hard and soft g oo ou, ow s, ss, c c, k, ck	1. Listen to the sounds some consonants make. 2. Does it look right? 3. Say and write. 4. Give it a go – Leave a blank! 5. Read aloud to proofread.

Creating Your Word List

In your notebook

- Make a list of 10 words you need to practise.
- Look at the letters you need to focus on.
- Use a coloured pencil to underline these letters. For example:

gentle cloud

- These are your Review Lesson Words.

Zoom in on Your Words

1. **Be a Slowpoke!** S...l...o...w...l...y say Lesson Words to yourself. Listen to each sound in the words.

2. **Scrunched-up Words** Write 5 or more Lesson Words together. Can a partner tell you the words you used?

togetherwoodenoutsidepencilsnack

3. **To get her in Together** Find and write smaller words in 3 Lesson Words. Ask a partner to find the smaller words.

4. **Rhyme Time** Choose 2 Lesson Words. For each, write 2 other words that rhyme. Circle patterns that stay the same.

> **flowers** sh(ow)ers t(ow)ers   **race** f(ace) base case

5. **Show a Word Another Way** Pick 1 Lesson Word. Draw a picture to show the word.

6. **Does It Look Right?** Trade Lesson Word lists with a partner. Write 3 of your partner's words 2 ways – 1 right and 1 wrong. Your partner circles the right spelling.

7. **Another Word for Nice** Synonyms are words that mean the same or almost the same thing. Pick 3 Lesson Words. Write a synonym for each. Look in a thesaurus if you need help.

8. **Ways to Sort** Write each Lesson Word on a piece of paper. Sort your words by:
   - pattern (fl**ow**ers, cl**ow**n),
   - sound (**gr**ass, **gr**ound), or
   - meaning (crawling, running).

   Ask a partner to look at your words and tell how you sorted.

9. **Read Aloud to Proofread** Read the Strategy Spot on page 91. Proofread a piece of writing you are working on or have just finished.

FLASHBACK

Which Lesson Words can you now spell? How can you use what you have learned to help you spell other words?

Look at this advertisement. How is the company trying to attract people to its store?

Word Box

noise
enjoy
oil
point
royal
coin
soil
voice
toys
boil

Creating Your Word List

Say these words:

What sound is the same in all of these words? Write the letters that make this sound.

1. Make a list of words that have the **oi** sound as in **toy**. The sound can be spelled **oi** or **oy**. You can use words from the advertisement to get started. List your words in a chart like this one.

oi	oy

2. With your teacher, list the words you will be learning to spell. You can use: the Word Box, the advertisement, your own words. These are your Lesson Words. Add these challenge words to your list:

hour, would

3. In your notebook
- Write your Lesson Words.
- Circle **oi** or **oy** in each word.

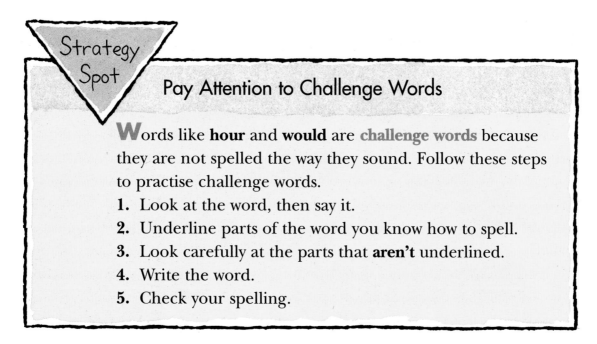

Strategy Spot

Pay Attention to Challenge Words

Words like **hour** and **would** are challenge words because they are not spelled the way they sound. Follow these steps to practise challenge words.
1. Look at the word, then say it.
2. Underline parts of the word you know how to spell.
3. Look carefully at the parts that **aren't** underlined.
4. Write the word.
5. Check your spelling.

Zoom in on Your Words

1. Pay Attention Pick 2 challenge words you need to practise. Use the Strategy Spot to help you learn the words.

2. Wordprints Look at these wordprints of 3 Word Box words. Write the words that match them in your notebook.

3. **Three of a Kind** The 2 words in each group have almost the same meaning. Add a Word Box word to make 3 words with the same or almost the same meaning. The first 1 has been done for you.

a) grand, noble, <u>r o y a l</u>

b) bangs, sounds, _ _ _ _ _ _

c) cook, heat, _ _ _ _

d) earth, dirt, _ _ _ _

4. **Oil Rhymes** Make words that rhyme with **oil**. Add the beginning consonants and blends to the **oil** pattern. Write the words in your notebook.

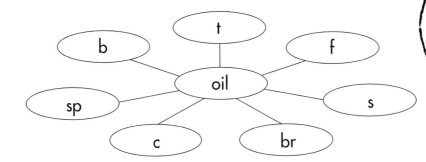

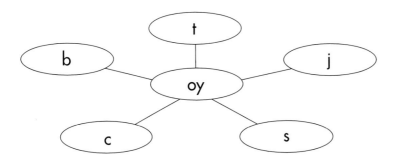

Oi is found at the beginning or middle of a word. **Oy** is found at the middle or end of a word.

QUICK TIP

5. **Oy Rhymes** Make words that rhyme with **oy**. Add the beginning consonants to the **oy** pattern. Write the words in your notebook.

6. **Draw a Noise** Boom is a loud noise. Whisper is a soft noise. List 5 loud noises in your house and 5 soft noises. Draw and label a noise of your choice.

FOCUS ON LANGUAGE ▷ Capital Letters

Capital letters are found in names, on signs, on labels, and in titles.

Other places you will find a capital letter are:
- at the start of every sentence (no matter how short it is),
- in short forms for provinces and states (ON, TX),
- in words an author wants you to read (THAT'S right).

Words that name a certain person, place, or thing always have a capital letter. These are called proper nouns. Examples are:
- a person's name (Anya Gordova),
- places – cities, towns, and countries (Dryden),
- things – rivers, lakes, and oceans (Sherbrooke Lake),
- brand names (Nike).

1. Write the names of 3 classmates.

2. Write the name of a river, a lake, and an ocean.

3. Write 3 brand names you know.

FLASHBACK

How can wordprint shapes help you learn to spell **oi** and **oy** words?

What do you see in your mind as you read "Balloons"?

Balloons

Balloons ballooning by

Billions of balloons
Quadrillions of balloons

Balloons bobbing

     bopping

        bouncing

           POPPING

High
(Good-bye)
Balloons

I watch until
My red balloon
   is
       swallowed
         by
           blue sky

Sheree Fitch

Word Box

riding

eating

giving

passing

reading

carrying

taking

trying

doing

hoping

Creating Your Word List

Say these words:

reading   riding   giving   carrying   hoping

What is the same about all of these words? Look at them again. What happens when **-ing** is added?

1. Make a list of words you know that have an **-ing** ending. Use the poem to get you started.

2. With your teacher, list the words you will be learning to spell. You can use: the Word Box, the poem, your own words. These are your Lesson Words.

3. **In your notebook**
   - Write your Lesson Words.
   - Say each word and underline the **-ing** ending.

Strategy Spot

Look for the Root Word

The main part of a word is called the **root** word. For example, root words of some Word Box words are *ride* and *carry*. When you want to spell a word, start with the root word. Then add the beginning and ending letters.

Zoom in on Your Words

1. **Show the Root** Write your Lesson Words. Underline the root word in each Lesson Word.

2. **Ballooning** Read the poem "Ballooning" again. What other words could you use that tell how a balloon moves? Write these words in a balloon shape.

3. **Connecting** In your notebook, write a Word Box word that completes each set.

   a) walking, swimming, _ _ _ _ _ _
   b) _ _ _ _ _ _ _ , speaking, writing
   c) presenting, providing, _ _ _ _ _ _
   d) grabbing, _ _ _ _ _ _ , snatching

4. **Make a Letter Ladder** Pick a Lesson Word. Write it in a row, from top to bottom. Use other Lesson Words to fill in the ladder.

```
      r e a d i n g
      t a k i n g
        t r y i n g
  h o p i n g
  d o i n g
        g i v i n g
```

5. **Learning About Root Words**

   Some root words change when you add **-ing** to them:

   jump + ing = jumping (no change)
   run + ing   = running (double final consonant)
   dine + ing = dining (drop silent e)

   Copy this chart in your notebook. Write Word Box words and your Lesson Words under the right heading.

No Change	Double Final Consonant	Drop Silent e

6. **Tidying** Make a list of things you do at home that end in **-ing** (washing dishes, picking up clothes). Bring your list to class.

FOCUS ON LANGUAGE ▷ Action Words – Verbs

A verb is a word that shows action – walk, skip, jump, ran, am.

> Gina and Leo **walk** to school together.
> I **am** here.

1. Which of these words are verbs?
   a) read   **b)** walk   **c)** corner   **d)** sign   **e)** swam

2. Look at "Ballooning" on page 100. Make a list of words that tell what balloons do.

3. Most verbs can take an **-ing** ending. Try adding **-ing** to these words. Write the verbs in your notebook.
   a) bounce   **b)** paper   **c)** stand   **d)** fork   **e)** type

4. Draw a picture that shows people doing things. Label the actions.

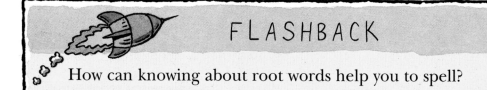

run running ran

Throw caught bounce

FLASHBACK

How can knowing about root words help you to spell?

Would you want one of these jobs?

Word Box

baker

river

under

farmer

better

winter

greater

number

paper

water

Creating Your Word List

Say these words:

Listen to the sound **-er** makes in these words. Is it the same sound in each word?

1. Make a list of words that end in **-er**. Use the names of the jobs in the want ads to get you started.

2. With your teacher, list the words you will be learning to spell. You can use: the Word Box, the want ads, your own words. These are your Lesson Words.

3. **In your notebook**
   - Write your Lesson Words.
   - Say each word and underline the **-er** ending.
   - Add words to your Personal Dictionary. This can help you in your reading and writing.

Know the Most Common Spelling

Different letter patterns can make the same sounds. Knowing the most common spelling can help you use the right spelling. This makes spelling easier. As you learn new words, pay attention to their patterns.

Zoom in on Your Words

1. **Baker Required**   Read the want ads in a newspaper. Choose a job you would like. Tell a partner why.

2. **Odd Word Out**   Read these groups of words. In your notebook, write the word that does **not** belong in each group.
   a) player, over, under
   b) paper, farmer, barber
   c) computer, larger, greater
   d) brother, teacher, mother

3. **From A to Z**   Find the group where words are not in alphabetical order. Write the words in your notebook in alphabetical order.
   a) baker, farmer, paper
   b) better, river, winter
   c) number, greater, water, under

Try This!   Write each Lesson Word on a small piece of paper. Put them in alphabetical order.

4. Word Pyramid Pick 3 Lesson Words you want to practise. In your notebook, make a word pyramid for each.

```
g
gr
gre
grea
great
greate
greater
```

Most times, when you hear **er**, it will be spelled **er**. Less often, it will be spelled **ar** or **or**.

QUICK TIP

5. Add -er to Make New Words When you add **-er** to the root of some words, you make new words. Look at these **-er** words.

Root + er		Makes
work + er	=	worker (a person who works)
print + er	=	printer (a person who prints, a machine that prints)
fast + er	=	faster (more quickly)

Look at your Lesson Words. Take off the **-er** ending. Do the remaining letters still make a word? (Remember that some root words drop an **e** or double a consonant when an ending is added.) How many of your Lesson Words are root words?

6. Job Search With a family member, list jobs you think you would like. Tell why.

FLASHBACK

What time do you usually do your At Home activity? Where is your favourite place to complete it?

106

Surveys

What would you like to be when you grow up? Imagine that you had the choice of being a baker, a farmer, or a teacher. What would you choose to be? Here is how 1 class chose jobs.

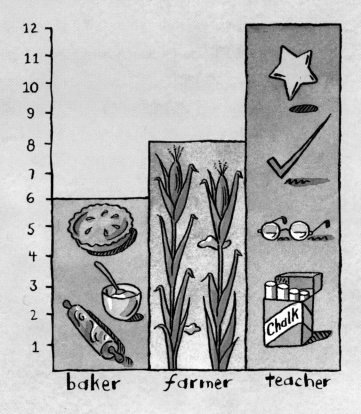

1. How many students wanted to be a baker? A farmer? A teacher?

2. Hold a class vote. Choose 1 job that you would like.

3. As a class, make a graph that shows each person's vote.

Many books have a note about the author. Here is a note about Loris Lesynski. You can see her work on pages 20 and 24.

Loris was born in Sweden. When she was two years old, her family moved to Toronto, Ontario. Loris knew very early in life that she wanted to write and illustrate children's books. Each poem and story that Loris writes goes through many drafts. For help, she reads her work to students at a local school. They tell her what they like and don't like. About her writing, Loris says, "I hope my poems, stories, and pictures will make kids laugh, and then make them say 'I like that. I think I'll write one of my own. Better than hers!'"

Word Box

cart
forget
return
first
afternoon
hurt
airport
hard
morning
north

Creating Your Word List

Say these words:

cart
afternoon
first
north
hurt

Listen to the sound each vowel makes when it is followed by **r**. Do **vowels + r** sound the same as long vowels? What about short vowels?

1. Make a list of words that have the **vowel + r** pattern. List your words in a chart like this one.

ar	er	ir	or	ur

2. With your teacher, list the words you will be learning to spell. You can use: the Word Box, the author note, your own words. These are your Lesson Words.

3. **In your notebook**
   - Write your Lesson Words.
   - Say each word and underline the **vowel + r**.

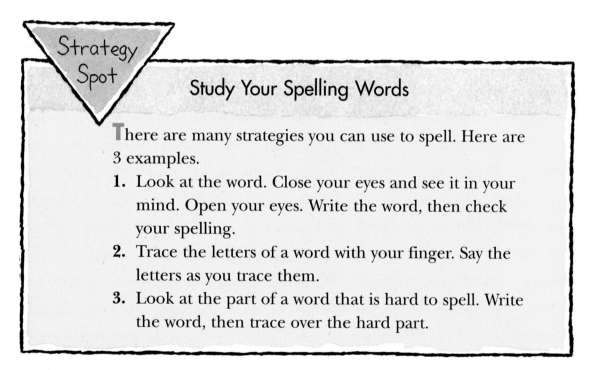

Strategy Spot

Study Your Spelling Words

There are many strategies you can use to spell. Here are 3 examples.

1. Look at the word. Close your eyes and see it in your mind. Open your eyes. Write the word, then check your spelling.
2. Trace the letters of a word with your finger. Say the letters as you trace them.
3. Look at the part of a word that is hard to spell. Write the word, then trace over the hard part.

Zoom in on Your Words

1. **Study Your Words** Study your Lesson Words using 1 of the strategies in the Strategy Spot.

2. **All About...** Write an author note about yourself. Include it at the end of the next story you write.

3. **Compound Words** Find the 2 compound words in the Word Box. Write them in your notebook. Underline the 2 words that make up each compound.

   Try This! Make up a new compound word for the 2 Word Box compounds.

4. **Partner Words** Think of partner words like *near* and *far*, *empty* and *full*. In your notebook, write a Word Box word to complete each pair of partner words.

   a) _ _ _ _ _ _ _ and night
   b) _ _ _ _ _ and south
   c) _ _ _ _ _ and last
   d) send and _ _ _ _ _ _

Many patterns can make the sound of **er** in **her** (w**or**m, f**ur**, **ear**th, doll**ar**).

QUICK TIP

5. **Word Chain** Work with a partner. Take turns writing Lesson Words and words from your Personal Dictionary to make a word chain. Try to make it as long as you can.

yar**d** **d**ir**t** **t**ur**n** **n**orth

6. **Book Jackets** Look at a book you are reading. What does it tell you about the story? What does it tell you about the author? Write 2 questions you would like to ask the author.

FLASHBACK

How would you help a friend who had trouble spelling Lesson Words?

SOCIAL STUDIES

Timelines

Author notes are 1 way to share information about a person. Another way is to make a timeline. A timeline includes information on important events in a person's life. It also tells when each event took place.

Imagine that someone wants to know all about your life. How could you show all of the information? Look at the timeline 1 grade 3 student made.

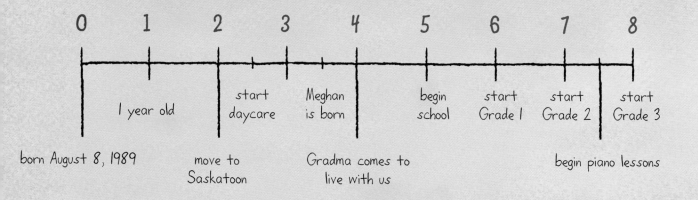

1. Write important events in your life in your notebook. Include when they happened.

2. Write the events in point form.

3. Draw your timeline. Make sure the space between each year is equal.

4. Start your timeline at 0. Number the timeline.

5. Write your events. You can also illustrate your timeline.

Look at this picture. There are 10 things whose names are spelled with a double consonant. Can you find them?

Word Box

sorry

dinner

swimming

happened

letter

jolly

tomorrow

summer

supper

kitten

Creating Your Word List

Say these words:

dinner   letter   supper   tomorrow   kitten

These words are the same in 2 ways. How are they the same?

1. Make a list of words you know that have double consonants. Use the picture to get you started.

2. With your teacher, list the words you will be learning to spell. You can use: the Word Box, the picture, your own words. These are your Lesson Words.

3. In your notebook

- Write your Lesson Words.
- Say each word and stress the double consonants.

Strategy Spot

Snap, Clap, and Tap Syllables

One way to spell long words is to divide them into smaller parts, or **syllables**. A syllable is a word part that has 1 vowel sound. Here is how the word **tomorrow** would be divided into syllables – to • mor • row. Follow these steps to find and spell syllables in a word.

1. Say the word to yourself.
2. Listen for each vowel sound.
3. Snap, clap, or tap each syllable.
4. Spell each syllable in order.

Zoom in on Your Words

1. **Snap, Clap, or Tap** Use the Strategy Spot steps to spell your Lesson Words.

2. **A Letter Home** In your notebook, write the Word Box words that complete these sentences.

   Well, so far nothing too exciting has _ _ _ _ _ _ _ _ at camp. We went _ _ _ _ _ _ _ _ yesterday, but that was before it rained. That's why I had the chance to write this _ _ _ _ _ _ . We will go horseback riding _ _ _ _ _ _ _ _ – I can hardly wait! I better finish. The _ _ _ _ _ _ bell is ringing. I hope everyone is well and that my new _ _ _ _ _ _ , Yellow, is also well.

3. **I Say Supper, You Say Pizza** Choose 1 Word Box word. Say it to a partner. Your partner says the word that your word made him or her think of. Take turns. Time yourself for 30 seconds. What were your first and last words?

4. **It happened ...** Use these starters to write sentences. Write them in your notebook.
   a) The kitten was ...   **b)** It happened ...
   c) He was sorry ...   **d)** Summer is ...

5. **Rob + -er, -ed, -ing** See what happens when **-er**, **-ed**, and **-ing** are added to **rob**. **Rob** has 1 syllable and 1 vowel (**o**) followed by 1 consonant (**b**). In a word like this, double the consonant when you add an ending. Look at a book you are reading. Find 5 words where a consonant has been doubled. Write the words in your notebook.

6. **Ball – Bell** Work with a partner. Make cards like these. Pick 5 consonants each. Take turns matching your consonants to the **vowel + ll** patterns. Write the words you were able to make.

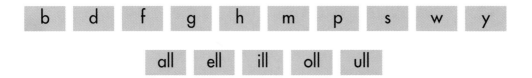

| b | d | f | g | h | m | p | s | w | y |

| all | ell | ill | oll | ull |

7. **Double Consonant Home** Look around your house. On a piece of paper, write the names of 5 things that have double consonants. Clap, tap, or snap the syllables in each word.

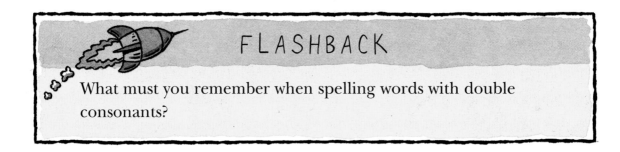

FLASHBACK

What must you remember when spelling words with double consonants?

Connecting with

ART

Picture Collages

A collage contains many pictures and things about 1 topic. Look at the picture at the top of page 112. It is a picture collage of things whose names contain double consonants. Here is how you can make a picture collage.

1. Pick a topic.

2. Look through old magazines and newspapers.

3. Cut out pictures about your topic.

4. Arrange your pictures on a large piece of paper.

5. Once you like how your collage looks, glue the pictures.

6. Give your collage a title. If you want, include some labels.

Patterns	Strategies
oi, oy -ing -er vowel + r double consonants	1. Pay attention to challenge words. 2. Look for the root word. 3. Know the most common spelling. 4. Study your spelling words. 5. Snap, clap, and tap syllables.

Creating Your Word List

In your notebook

- Make a list of 10 words you need to practise.
- Look at the letters you need to focus on.
- Use a coloured pencil to underline these letters. For example:

return   tomorrow

- These are your Review Lesson Words.

Zoom in on Your Words

1. **Be a Slowpoke!** S...l...o...w...l...y say Lesson Words to yourself. Listen to each sound in the words.

2. **Snap, Clap, Tap** Find your 3 longest Lesson Words. Snap, clap, or tap each syllable in the words.

3. **Find the Verbs** Choose 1 verb from your Lesson Word list. Draw a picture to show what it means.

4. **Word Chain** Write 1 Lesson Word. Write another Lesson Word that begins with the last letter of the first word. When you run out of Lesson Words, use other words you know.

blanket trying greater river

5. **Compound Words** Have you included compound words in your list? If you answered yes, underline the 2 words that make each compound word.

6. **Word Association** Choose 1 Lesson Word. Say it to a partner. Your partner says the word that your word makes him or her think of. Take turns. Time yourself for 30 seconds. What were your first and last words?

7. **Root Words** Find out which of your Lesson Words are root words. Add **-ing** or **-er** to each word. Can the word take 1 or both endings? Make a chart with these heads. Write your Lesson Words and the words they can make. An example has been done for you.

Root Word	-ing	-er
hurt	hurting	____

8. **Study Your Spelling Words** Choose 3 Lesson Words you need to practise. Use 1 of the Spelling Strategies on page 109 to learn the words.

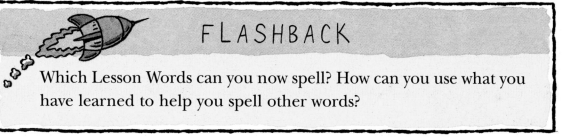

FLASHBACK

Which Lesson Words can you now spell? How can you use what you have learned to help you spell other words?

Match these picture pairs to the words pairs. Write them in your notebook.

a)

b)

c)

d)

1. plain – fancy   2. big – little
3. under – over   4. fast – slow

Word Box

heavy
crunch
myself
watch
forest
blanket
maybe
sometime
softly
useful

Creating Your Word List

Say these words:

watch   maybe   sometime
heavy   useful

What vowel sounds do you hear in the words? Is there more than 1 way to spell the same sound?

1. Make a list of words that have different patterns for spelling the same vowel sound (try, lie).

2. With your teacher, list the words you will be learning to spell. You can use: the Word Box, the picture pairs, your own words. These are your Lesson Words.

3. **In your notebook**
   - Write your Lesson Words.
   - Say each word and listen to the vowel sounds.
   - Underline the pattern for each vowel sound.
   - Add words to your Personal Dictionary. This can help you in your reading and writing.

Hear How Some Vowel Patterns Make the Same Sound

Some vowel patterns, like **ou** and **ow**, make the same sound. When you are not sure what vowel pattern to use, write the word several ways. Look at both words. Choose the 1 that looks right. It probably is.

Zoom in on Your Words

1. **T _ d for First Pr _ ze** Trade Lesson Word lists with a partner. Pick 5 of your partner's Lesson Words. Replace long vowel sounds with a dash (_). Your partner fills in the vowel sounds.

2. **Get in Shape** Pick 5 Lesson Words. Draw the wordprint shapes for them in your notebook. Write the letters for each word.

Try This! Trade Lesson Word lists with a partner. Draw wordprint shapes for 3 words. Match the shapes with the words.

3. **Vowels and Sounds**   Copy this chart in your notebook. Add your Lesson Words to it.

Word	Vowels I See	Vowel Sounds I Hear
heavy anything	e, a, y a, y, i	short e, long e short e, long e, short i

4. **Sometime...**   Use these starters to write sentences. Write them in your notebook.
   a) Softly, the horse...   **b)** The silver watch...   **c)** A crunch...

5. **Write and Sort**   Write each Lesson Word on a small piece of paper. Think about ways to sort words, for example, by pattern, meaning, or sound. Give your sorted words to a partner. Can she or he tell how you sorted them?

Did You Know ?

The pattern **ea** can make 3 vowel sounds – **long e**, **long a**, and **short e**.

6. **Vowel Collage**   Pick a topic like long or short vowels. Look through old newspapers and magazines. Cut out pictures of 5 things whose names have that sound. Paste the pictures on a piece of paper and print their names.

FLASHBACK

What vowel sound is easy to spell?

FOCUS ON LANGUAGE  Words that Mean the Opposite – Antonyms

Antonyms are words that mean the opposite. **Young** is the opposite of **old**.
Winter is the opposite of **summer**. Look at the picture pairs on page 118.
Each is a set of antonyms.

1. In your notebook, write the antonym for each word.
   a) hot   **b)** tall   **c)** happy   **d)** empty   **e)** excited

2. Some words can be made into antonyms when **un-**, **dis-**, or **mis-** is
added to a word. Look at these antonym pairs.

   eaten – uneaten   appear – disappear   behave – misbehave

Look in a newspaper or book. Find 5 words that have **un-**, **dis-**, or **mis-**
added to the front of a word.

3. Read this sentence: Long is to short as big is to small. **Long** and **short**
are antonyms, and **big** and **small** are antonyms. In your notebook,
write the antonym that fits these sentences.

   a) Smile is to _____ as happy is to sad. (frown, laugh,
   joyful)

   b) _____ is to found as give is to keep. (save, lost, take)

How many sentences can you make from these words?

the	honest	knights	climb
is	knobby	ghosts	talks
are	frightful	lamb	catches
and	naughty	calf	knock

Word Box

whole
walk
writing
couldn't
sword
eight
knot
castle
caught
lamb

Creating Your Word List

Say these words:

What is the same about all of these words? Which consonants are seen but not heard?

1. Make a list of words that have silent consonants. Use the words at the top of the page to get started. Write your words in a chart like this one.

Silent w	Silent l	Silent t	Silent b	others

2. With your teacher, list the words you will be learning to spell. You can use: the Word Box, the words on page 122, your own words. These are your Lesson Words.

3. **In your notebook**
   - Write your Lesson Words.
   - Say each word.
   - Underline the silent consonants in each word.

Strategy Spot

Highlight Letters that Need Attention

Sometimes we can spell most of a word, but get stuck on 1 or 2 letters. You can highlight these letters so that you pay extra attention to them.

1. Stress the problem letters when you say the word aloud.
2. Write the word. Underline the problem letters.

Zoom in on Your Words

1. **Highlight Letters** Write your Lesson Words. Highlight letters that make the words hard to spell.

2. **Wordprints** Match the Word Box words to these wordprints.

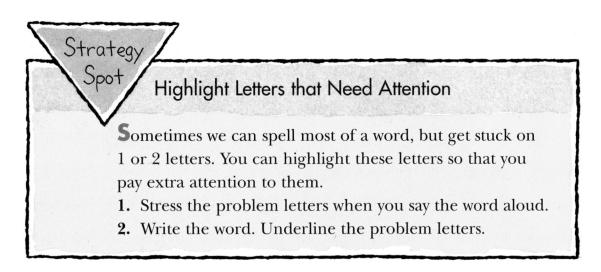

Try This! Make wordprints for other Word Box words. Can a partner tell you the words that match the prints?

3. **Three of a Kind** Read each set of words. Find a Word Box word that could be added to a set to make 3 of a kind. Write the words in your notebook.

 a) quarter, half, _ _ _ _ _
 b) crawl, _ _ _ _ , run
 c) wouldn't, _ _ _ _ _ _ ' _ , shouldn't
 d) six, seven, _ _ _ _ _
 e) catch, catching, _ _ _ _ _ _
 f) calf, kitten, _ _ _ _

4. **Stress It!** Write your Lesson Words on a piece of paper. Make silent consonants bigger than other letters. Say each word. Stress the silent consonant. For example, say **k - nee** for **knee**.

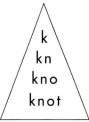

k-nee

5. **_ onest** Trade Lesson Word lists with a partner. Write the words, but leave a dash for silent consonants. Your partner writes the silent consonant to complete the word.

6. **Word Pyramids** Make word pyramids for Lesson Words you want to practise.

k
kn
kno
knot

7. **The Word Inside** Find smaller words in these larger words. Write the words in your notebook.

 a) frighten
 b) eighteen
 c) written
 d) laughter
 e) climbing
 f) thumb

Try This! Mix the order of letters to make even more words.

8. **Jona🗙** Make a list of names of family and friends. Put an X through silent consonants.

124

FOCUS ON LANGUAGE ▷ Sentences

Most sentences have a noun and a verb. Nouns are naming words. They name a person, place, or thing. Verbs are action words. They tell the actions of a noun – what the person, place, or thing is doing. For more about nouns and verbs, see page 63 and 103.

1. Look at the two pictures. Write a sentence for each. Underline the noun and circle the verb.

2. In most sentences, the noun is first. Look at these out-of-order sentences. In your notebook, write the words in order to make a sentence. Underline each noun and circle each verb.
   a) the ran bear quickly.   **b)** talked Stacey for 2 hours.
   c) is she going.   **c)** the cheered town for joy.

3. In your notebook, make a star (*) beside the sentence in #2 that can ask a question.

4. Look through a piece of your writing. Lightly underline the nouns and circle the verbs you used in 1 paragraph. Trade paragraphs with a partner. Can she or he find other nouns and verbs?

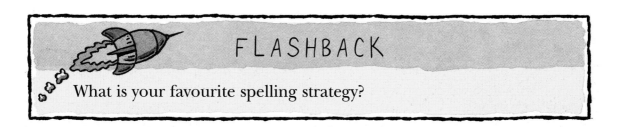

FLASHBACK

What is your favourite spelling strategy?

Word List

Words printed in **bold** are **challenge words**.

A

across 22
afraid 7
afternoon 28
age 7
airport 28
almost 10
also 10
another 13
anything 13
around 21

B

baker 27
baseball 22
beautiful 7
began 19
better 27
blanket 31
blend 2
block 2
blow 2
blue 11
boil 25
bought 17
bright 17
broom 20
brought 17
brush 15

C

cage 7
carry 23
carrying 26
cart 28
castle 32
catch 16
caught 32

cents 22
chain 7
chair 16
chalk 16
cheese 16
chicken 16
child 9
children 16
choice 16
class 22
clear 2
climb 9
close 2
clothes 10
cloud 21
clown 21
clue 2
coach 16
coin 25
colour 23
comb 10
cookies 20
cost 1
could 23
couldn't 32
count 21
cracker 23
crawl 3
crowd 3
crunch 31

D

desk 4
dinner 29
dishes 15
doctor 23
doing 26
downstairs 21

dragon 19
drift 1

E

earth 13
eating 26
eight 32
enjoy 25
even 8
everything . . . 13

F

farmer 27
finish 15
first 28
flame 2
flies 2
flip 2
floor 2
flowers 21
follow 10
food 20
forest 31
forget 28
friend 3
frost 3

G

garden 19
gather 19
gentle 19
giant 19
giving 26
golden 10
grade 7
grandmother . 3
grass 3
greater 27

grew 11
ground 3
guess 7

H

happened 29
hard 28
heavy 31
high 9
hope 10
hoping 26
hour 25
huge 11
hurt 28

I

inside 9

J

jolly 29
June 11

K

kept 23
kind 9
kitten 29
knees 8
knife 17
knight 17
knot 32
know 17

L

lamb 32
large 19
leaf 8
letter 29
lies 9

126